THE BEST OF
A.W. TOZER

D0172422

THE BEST OF
A.W. TOZER

52 FAVORITE CHAPTERS

Compiled by

WARREN W. WIERSBE

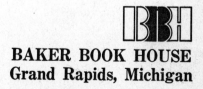

BAKER BOOK HOUSE
Grand Rapids, Michigan

Contents

Excerpts from
Of God and Men

Excerpts from
Man: The Dwelling Place of God

Excerpt from
How to Be Filled with the Holy Spirit

Excerpt from
Worship: The Missing Jewel of the Evangelical Church

Excerpt from
Who Put Jesus on the Cross?

Excerpt from
Paths to Power

Excerpt from
Let My People Go

Introduction

"I guess my philosophy is this: Everything is wrong until God sets it right."

That statement from Dr. A. W. Tozer perfectly summarizes what he believed and what he tried to do during his years of ministry. The entire focus of his preaching and writing was on God. He had no time for religious hucksters who were inventing new ways to promote their wares and inflate their statistics. Like Thoreau, whom he read and admired, Tozer marched to a different drummer; and for this reason, he was usually out of step with many of the people in the religious parade.

But it was this evangelical eccentricity that made us love him and appreciate him. He was not afraid to tell us what was wrong. Nor was he hesitant to tell us how God could make it right. If a sermon can be compared to light, then A. W. Tozer released a laser beam from the pulpit, a beam that penetrated your heart, seared your conscience, exposed sin, and left you crying, "What must I do to be saved?" The answer was always the same: surrender to Christ; get to know God personally; grow to become like Him.

Aiden Wilson Tozer was born in Newburg (then known as La Jose), Pennsylvania, on April 21, 1897. In 1912 the family moved from the farm to Akron, Ohio; and in 1915 he was converted to Christ. He immediately entered into a life of devotional intensity and personal witness. In 1919 he began pastoring the Alliance Church in Nutter Fort, West Virginia. He also pastored churches in Morgantown, West Virginia; Toledo, Ohio; Indianapolis, Indiana; and in 1928 came to the Southside Alliance Church in Chicago. Here he ministered until November, 1959, when he became pastor of the Avenue Road Church in Toronto. A sudden heart attack on May 12, 1963, ended that ministry and Tozer was ushered into Glory.

I am sure that Tozer reached more people through his writing than his preaching. Much of his writing was reflected in the preaching of pastors who fed their souls on his words. In May, 1950, he was named editor of *The Alliance Weekly*, now *The Alliance Witness*, which was probably the only religious magazine purchased primarily for its editorials. I once heard Dr. Tozer at an Evangelical Press Association conference taking to task editors who practiced what he called "super-market journalism—two columns of advertising and one aisle of reading material." He was an exacting writer and was as hard on himself as he was on others.

What is there about A. W. Tozer's writings that gets hold of us and will not let us go? Tozer did not enjoy the privilege of a university or seminary training, or even a Bible School education for that matter; yet he has left us a shelf of books that will be mined for their spiritual wealth until the Lord returns.

For one thing, A. W. Tozer wrote with conviction. He was not interested in tickling the ears of the shallow Athenian Christians who were looking for some new thing. Tozer redug the old wells and called us back to the old paths, and he passionately believed and practiced the truths that he taught. He once told a friend of mine, "I have preached myself off of every Bible Conference platform in the country!" The popular crowds do not rush to hear a man whose convictions make them uncomfortable.

Tozer was a mystic—an evangelical mystic—in an age that is pragmatic and materialistic. He still calls us to see that real world of the spiritual that lies beyond the physical world that so ensnares us. He begs us to please God and forget the crowd. He implores us to worship God that we might become more like Him. How desperately we need that message today!

A. W. Tozer had the gift of taking a spiritual truth and holding it up to the light so that, like a diamond, every facet was seen and admired. He was not lost in homiletical swamps; the wind of the Spirit blew and dead bones came to life. His essays are like fine cameos whose value is not determined by their size. His preaching was characterized by an intensity—spiritual intensity—that penetrated one's heart and helped him to see God. Happy is the Christian who has a Tozer book handy when his soul is parched and he feels God is far away.

This leads to what I think is the greatest contribution A. W. Tozer makes in his writings: he so excites you about truth that you forget Tozer and reach for your Bible. He himself often said that the best book is the one that makes you want to put it down and think for yourself. Rarely do I read Tozer without reaching for my notebook to jot down some truth that later can be developed into a message. Tozer is like a prism that gathers the light and then reveals its beauty.

To select "the best of A. W. Tozer" is an impossible task. Best for whom? For what needs? As a pastor, I could select fifty essays that would challenge and bless the hearts of my brothers in the ministry, but Tozer is read by many people who are not pastors. As a writer, I could choose chapters from his books that reveal his skill with words; but most readers are not writers. Those of us who appreciate Tozer's writings certainly have our favorites, but no two of us would agree.

From the Tozer books published by Christian Publications of Harrisburg, Pennsylvania, I have made selections on the basis of theme and development. Dr. Tozer often said the same things in different ways, and I have tried to choose major themes in their best expression. If one of your favorite essays is missing, perhaps you will be compensated by reading a new one that you have missed or forgotten.

If this book is your first introduction to A. W. Tozer, then permit me to suggest the best way to read these essays. Please read them slowly and meditatively, thinking as you read. Do not "speed read" these chapters. As you read, listen for what Tozer called "the other Voice" speaking truth through these brief messages. If a certain truth begins to burn in your soul, put the book down and let God instruct you by His Spirit. Wait quietly before Him and deep within your heart God will speak to you.

"The best book is not one that informs merely," Tozer wrote in *Man: The Dwelling Place of God*, "but one that stirs the reader up to inform himself."

I trust that this book, composed of what I think are the best of Tozer's writings, will meet that standard. I think that it will. I pray that it will introduce a host of new readers to the writings of this man of God, and that those of us who have known him longer will appreciate him more.

Warren W. Wiersbe
The Moody Church
Chicago, Illinois

Excerpts from
The Pursuit of God

Following Hard After God
The Speaking Voice
Meekness and Rest

1

Following Hard After God

My soul followeth hard after thee:
thy right hand upholdeth me.

Ps. 63:8

Christian theology teaches the doctrine of prevenient grace, which briefly stated means this, that before a man can seek God, God must first have sought the man.

Before a sinful man can think a right thought of God, there must have been a work of enlightenment done within him; imperfect it may be, but a true work nonetheless, and the secret cause of all desiring and seeking and praying which may follow.

We pursue God because, and only because, He has first put an urge within us that spurs us to the pursuit. "No man can come to me," said our Lord, "except the Father which hath sent me draw him," and it is by this very prevenient *drawing* that God takes from us every vestige of credit for the act of coming. The impulse to pursue God originates with God, but the outworking of that impulse is our following hard after Him; and all the time we are pursuing Him we are already in His hand: "Thy right hand upholdeth me."

In this divine "upholding" and human "following" there is no contradiction. All is of God, for as von Hugel teaches, *God is always previous*. In practice, however, (that is, where God's previous working meets man's present response) man must pursue God. On our part there must be positive reciprocation if this secret drawing of God is to eventuate in identifiable experience of the Divine. In the warm language of personal feeling this is

stated in the Forty-second Psalm: "As the hart panteth after the water brooks, so panteth my soul after thee, O
God. My soul thirsteth for God, for the living God: when
shall I come and appear before God?" This is deep calling
unto deep, and the longing heart will understand it.

The doctrine of justification by faith—a Biblical truth,
and a blessed relief from sterile legalism and unavailing
self-effort—has in our time fallen into evil company and
been interpreted by many in such manner as actually to
bar men from the knowledge of God. The whole transaction of religious conversion has been made mechanical and
spiritless. Faith may now be exercised without a jar to the
moral life and without embarrassment to the Adamic ego.
Christ may be "received" without creating any special
love for Him in the soul of the receiver. The man is
"saved," but he is not hungry nor thirsty after God. In
fact he is specifically taught to be satisfied and encouraged
to be content with little.

The modern scientist has lost God amid the wonders of
His world; we Christians are in real danger of losing God
amid the wonders of His Word. We have almost forgotten
that God is a Person and, as such, can be cultivated as any
person can. It is inherent in personality to be able to know
other personalities, but full knowledge of one personality
by another cannot be achieved in one encounter. It is only
after long and loving mental intercourse that the full pos-
sibilities of both can be explored.

All social intercourse between human beings is a response of personality to personality, grading upward from
the most casual brush between man and man to the full-
est, most intimate communion of which the human soul is
capable. Religion, so far as it is genuine, is in essence the
response of created personalities to the Creating Personality, God. "This is life eternal, that they might know thee
the only true God, and Jesus Christ, whom thou hast
sent."

God is a Person, and in the deep of His mighty nature

He thinks, wills, enjoys, feels, loves, desires and suffers as any other person may. In making Himself known to us, He stays by the familiar pattern of personality. He communicates with us through the avenues of our minds, our wills and our emotions. The continuous and unembarrassed interchange of love and thought between God and the soul of the redeemed man is the throbbing heart of New Testament religion.

This intercourse between God and the soul is known to us in conscious personal awareness. It is personal: that is, it does not come through the body of believers, as such, but is known to the individual, and to the body through the individuals which compose it. And it is conscious: that is, it does not stay below the threshold of consciousness and work there unknown to the soul (as, for instance, infant baptism is thought by some to do), but comes within the field of awareness where the man can "know" it as he knows any other fact of experience.

You and I are in little (our sins excepted) what God is in large. Being made in His image we have within us the capacity to know Him. In our sins we lack only the power. The moment the Spirit has quickened us to life in regeneration our whole being senses its kinship to God and leaps up in joyous recognition. That is the heavenly birth without which we cannot see the Kingdom of God. It is, however, not an end but an inception, for now begins the glorious pursuit, the heart's happy exploration of the infinite riches of the Godhead. That is where we begin, I say, but where we stop no man has yet discovered, for there is in the awful and mysterious depths of the Triune God neither limit nor end.

> *Shoreless Ocean, who can sound Thee?*
> *Thine own eternity is round Thee,*
> *Majesty divine!*

To have found God and still to pursue Him is the soul's

paradox of love, scorned indeed by the too-easily-satisfied religionist, but justified in happy experience by the children of the burning heart. St. Bernard stated this holy paradox in a musical quatrain that will be instantly understood by every worshiping soul:

> We taste Thee, O Thou Living Bread,
>   And long to feast upon Thee still:
> We drink of Thee, the Fountainhead
>   And thirst our souls from Thee to fill.

Come near to the holy men and women of the past and you will soon feel the heat of their desire after God. They mourned for Him, they prayed and wrestled and sought for Him day and night, in season and out, and when they had found Him the finding was all the sweeter for the long seeking. Moses used the fact that he knew God as an argument for knowing Him better. "Now, therefore, I pray thee, if I have found grace in thy sight, show me now thy way, that I may know thee, that I may find grace in thy sight"; and from there he rose to make the daring request, "I beseech thee, show me thy glory." God was frankly pleased by this display of ardor, and the next day called Moses into the mount, and there in solemn procession made all His glory pass before him.

David's life was a torrent of spiritual desire, and his psalms ring with the cry of the seeker and the glad shout of the finder. Paul confessed the mainspring of his life to be his burning desire after Christ. "That I may know Him," was the goal of his heart, and to this he sacrificed everything. "Yea doubtless, and I count all things but loss for the excellency of the knowledge of Christ Jesus my Lord: for whom I have suffered the loss of all things, and do count them but refuse, that I may win Christ."

Hymnody is sweet with the longing after God, the God whom, while the singer seeks, he knows he has already found. "His track I see and I'll pursue," sang our fathers only a short generation ago, but that song is heard no more in the great congregation. How tragic that we in this dark day have had our seeking done for us by our teachers. Everything is made to center upon the initial act of "accepting" Christ (a term, incidentally, which is not found in the Bible) and we are not expected thereafter to crave any further revelation of God to our souls. We have been snared in the coils of a spurious logic which insists that if we have found Him we need no more seek Him. This is set before us as the last word in orthodoxy, and it is taken for granted that no Bible-taught Christian ever believed otherwise. Thus the whole testimony of the worshiping, seeking, singing Church on that subject is crisply set aside. The experiential heart-theology of a grand army of fragrant saints is rejected in favor of a smug interpretation of Scripture which would have sounded strange to an Augustine, a Rutherford or a Brainerd.

In the midst of this great chill, there are some I rejoice to acknowledge, who will not be content with shallow logic. They will admit the force of the argument, and then turn away with tears to hunt some lonely place and pray, "O God, show me thy glory." They want to taste, to touch with their hearts, to see with their inner eyes the wonder that is God.

I want deliberately to encourage this mighty longing after God. The lack of it has brought us to our present low estate. The stiff and wooden quality about our religious lives is a result of our lack of holy desire. Complacency is a deadly foe of all spiritual growth. Acute desire must be present or there will be no manifestation of Christ to His people. He waits to be wanted. Too bad that with many of us He waits so long, so very long, in vain.

Every age has its own characteristics. Right now we are in an age of religious complexity. The simplicity which is in Christ is rarely found among us. In its stead are programs, methods, organizations and a world of nervous activities which occupy time and attention but can never satisfy the longing of the heart. The shallowness of our inner experience, the hollowness of our worship, and that servile imitation of the world which marks our promotional methods all testify that we, in this day, know God only imperfectly, and the peace of God scarcely at all.

If we would find God amid all the religious externals we must first determine to find Him, and then proceed in the way of simplicity. Now, as always, God reveals Himself to "babes" and hides Himself in thick darkness from the wise and the prudent. We must simplify our approach to Him. We must strip down to essentials (and they will be found to be blessedly few). We must put away all effort to impress, and come with the guileless candor of childhood. If we do this, without doubt God will quickly respond.

When religion has said its last word, there is little that we need other than God Himself. The evil habit of seeking *God-and* effectively prevents us from finding God in full revelation. In the "and" lies our great woe. If we omit the "and," we shall soon find God, and in Him we shall find that for which we have all our lives been secretly longing.

We need not fear that in seeking God only we may narrow our lives or restrict the motions of our expanding hearts. The opposite is true. We can well afford to make God our All, to concentrate, to sacrifice the many for the One.

The author of the quaint old English classic, *The Cloud of Unknowing,* teaches us how to do this. "Lift up thine heart unto God with a meek stirring of love; and mean Himself, and none of His goods. And thereto, look thee loath to think on aught but God Himself. So that nought work in thy wit, nor in thy will, but only God Himself. This is the work of the soul that most pleaseth God."

Again, he recommends that in prayer we practice a further stripping down of everything, even of our theology. "For it sufficeth enough, a naked intent direct unto God without any other cause than Himself." Yet underneath all his thinking lay the broad foundation of New Testament truth, for he explains that by "Himself" he means "God that made thee, and bought thee, and that graciously called thee to thy degree." And he is all for simplicity: If we would have religion "lapped and folden in one word, for that thou shouldst have better hold thereupon, take thee but a little word of one syllable: for so it is better than of two, for even the shorter it is the better it accordeth with the work of the Spirit. And such a word is this word GOD or this word LOVE."

When the Lord divided Canaan among the tribes of Israel, Levi received no share of the land. God said to him simply, "I am thy part and thine inheritance," and by those words made him richer than all his brethren, richer than all the kings and rajas who have ever lived in the world. And there is a spiritual principle here, a principle still valid for every priest of the Most High God.

The man who has God for his treasure has all things in One. Many ordinary treasures may be denied him, or if he is allowed to have them, the enjoyment of them will be so tempered that they will never be necessary to his happiness. Or if he must see them go, one after one, he will scarcely feel a sense of loss, for having the Source of all things he has in One all satisfaction, all pleasure, all delight. Whatever he may lose, he has actually lost nothing, for he now has it all in One, and he has it purely, legitimately and forever.

O God, I have tasted Thy goodness, and it has both satisfied me and made me thirsty for more. I am painfully conscious of my need of further grace. I am ashamed of my lack of desire. O God, the Triune God, I want to want Thee; I long to be filled with longing; I thirst to be made more thirsty still. Show me Thy glory, I pray Thee, that so I may know Thee indeed. Begin in mercy a new work of love within me. Say to my soul, "Rise up, my love, my fair one, and come away." Then give me grace to rise and follow Thee up from this misty lowland where I have wandered so long. In Jesus' Name, Amen.

2

The Speaking Voice

*In the beginning was the Word,
and the Word was with God, and
the Word was God.*

John 1:1

An intelligent plain man, untaught in the truths of Christianity, coming upon this text, would likely conclude that John meant to teach that it is the nature of God to speak, to communicate His thoughts to others. And he would be right. A word is a medium by which thoughts are expressed, and the application of the term to the Eternal Son leads us to believe that self-expression is inherent in the Godhead, that God is forever seeking to speak Himself out to His creation. The whole Bible supports the idea. God is speaking. Not God spoke, but *God is speaking*. He is by His nature continuously articulate. He fills the world with His speaking Voice.

One of the great realities with which we have to deal is the Voice of God in His world. The briefest and only satisfying cosmogony is this: "He spake and it was done." The *why* of natural law is the living Voice of God immanent in His creation. And this word of God which brought all worlds into being cannot be understood to mean the Bible, for it is not a written or printed word at all, but the expression of the will of God spoken into the structure of all things. This word of God is the breath of God filling the world with living potentiality. The Voice of God is the most powerful force in nature, indeed the only force in nature, for all energy is here only because the power-filled Word is being spoken.

The Bible is the written word of God, and because it is

written it is confined and limited by the necessities of ink and paper and leather. The Voice of God, however, is alive and free as the sovereign God is free. "The words that I speak unto you, they are spirit, and they are life." The life is in the speaking words. God's word in the Bible can have power only because it corresponds to God's word in the universe. It is the present Voice which makes the written Word all-powerful. Otherwise it would lie locked in slumber within the covers of a book.

We take a low and primitive view of things when we conceive of God at the creation coming into physical contact with things, shaping and fitting and building like a carpenter. The Bible teaches otherwise: "By the word of the Lord were the heavens made; and all the host of them by the breath of his mouth. . . . For he spake, and it was done; he commanded, and it stood fast." "Through faith we understand that the worlds were framed by the word of God." Again we must remember that God is referring here not to His written Word, but to His speaking Voice. His world-filling Voice is meant, that Voice which antedates the Bible by uncounted centuries, that Voice which has not been silent since the dawn of creation, but is sounding still throughout the full far reaches of the universe.

The Word of God is quick and powerful. In the beginning He spoke to nothing, and it became *something*. Chaos heard it and became order, darkness heard it and became light. "And God said—and it was so." These twin phrases, as cause and effect, occur throughout the Genesis story of the creation. The *said* accounts for the *so*. The *so* is the *said* put into the continuous present.

That God is here and that He is speaking—these truths are back of all other Bible truths; without them there could be no revelation at all. God did not write a book and send it by messenger to be read at a distance by unaided minds. He spoke a Book and lives in His spoken words, constantly speaking His words and causing the power of

them to persist across the years. God breathed on clay and
it became a man; He breathes on men and they become
clay. "Return ye children of men," was the word spoken
at the Fall by which God decreed the death of every man,
and no added word has He needed to speak. The sad procession of mankind across the face of the earth from birth
to the grave is proof that His original Word was enough.

We have not given sufficient attention to that deep ut-
terance in the Book of John, "That was the true Light,
which lighteth every man that cometh into the world."
Shift the punctuation around as we will and the truth is
still there: the Word of God affects the hearts of all men
as light in the soul. In the hearts of all men the light
shines, the Word sounds, and there is no escaping them.
Something like this would of necessity be so if God is
alive and in His world. And John says that it is so. Even
those persons who have never heard of the Bible have still
been preached to with sufficient clarity to remove every excuse from their hearts forever. "Which show the work of
the law written in their hearts, their conscience also bearing witness, and their thoughts the meanwhile either ac-
cusing or else excusing one another." "For the invisible
things of him from the creation of the world are clearly
seen, being understood by the things that are made, even
his eternal power and Godhead; so that they are without
excuse."

This universal Voice of God was by the ancient Hebrews often called Wisdom, and was said to be everywhere sounding and searching throughout the earth,
seeking some response from the sons of men. The eighth
chapter of the Book of Proverbs begins, "Doth not wisdom cry? and understanding put forth her voice?" The
writer then pictures wisdom as a beautiful woman standing "in the top of the high places, by the way in the
places of the paths." She sounds her voice from every
quarter so that no one may miss hearing it. "Unto you, O
men, I call; and my voice is to the sons of men." Then she

pleads for the simple and the foolish to give ear to her words. It is spiritual response for which this Wisdom of God is pleading, a response which she has always sought and is but rarely able to secure. The tragedy is that our eternal welfare depends upon our hearing, and we have trained our ears not to hear.

This universal Voice has ever sounded, and it has often troubled men even when they did not understand the source of their fears. Could it be that this Voice distilling like a living mist upon the hearts of men has been the un-discovered cause of the troubled conscience and the long-ing for immortality confessed by millions since the dawn of recorded history? We need not fear to face up to this. The speaking Voice is a fact. How men have reacted to it is for any observer to note.

When God spoke out of heaven to our Lord, self-cen-tered men who heard it explained it by natural causes: they said, "It thundered." This habit of explaining the Voice by appeals to natural law is at the very root of mod-ern science. In the living, breathing cosmos there is a mys-terious Something, too wonderful, too awful for any mind to understand. The believing man does not claim to under-stand. He falls to his knees and whispers, "God." The man of earth kneels also, but not to worship. He kneels to examine, to search, to find the cause and the how of things. Just now we happen to be living in a secular age. Our thought habits are those of the scientist, not those of the worshiper. We are more likely to explain than to adore. "It thundered," we exclaim, and go our earthly way. But still the Voice sounds and searches. The order and life of the world depend upon that Voice, but men are mostly too busy or too stubborn to give attention.

Everyone of us has had experiences which we have not been able to explain: a sudden sense of loneliness, or a feeling of wonder or awe in the face of the universal vastness. Or we have had a fleeting visitation of light like an illumination from some other sun, giving us in a quick flash an assurance that we are from another world, that our origins are divine. What we saw there, or felt, or heard, may have been contrary to all that we had been taught in the schools and at wide variance with all our former beliefs and opinions. We were forced to suspend our acquired doubts while, for a moment, the clouds were rolled back and we saw and heard for ourselves. Explain such things as we will, I think we have not been fair to the facts until we allow at least the possibility that such experiences may arise from the Presence of God in the world and His persistent effort to communicate with mankind. Let us not dismiss such an hypothesis too flippantly.

It is my own belief (and here I shall not feel bad if no one follows me) that every good and beautiful thing which man has produced in the world has been the result of his faulty and sin-blocked response to the creative Voice sounding over the earth. The moral philosophers who dreamed their high dreams of virtue, the religious thinkers who speculated about God and immortality, the poets and artists who created out of common stuff pure and lasting beauty: how can we explain them? It is not enough to say simply, "It was genius." What then is genius? Could it be that a genius is a man haunted by the speaking Voice, laboring and striving like one possessed to achieve ends which he only vaguely understands? That the great man may have missed God in his labors, that he may even have spoken or written against God does not destroy the idea I am advancing. God's redemptive revelation in the Holy Scriptures is necessary to saving faith and peace with God. Faith in a risen Saviour is necessary if the vague stirrings toward immortality are to bring us to restful and satisfying communion with God. To me this is a plausible explanation of all that is best out of Christ. But you can be a good Christian and not accept my thesis.

The Voice of God is a friendly Voice. No one need fear to listen to it unless he has already made up his mind to resist it. The blood of Jesus has covered not only the human race but all creation as well. "And having made peace through the blood of his cross, by him to reconcile all things unto himself; by him, I say, whether they be things in earth, or things in heaven." We may safely preach a friendly Heaven. The heaven as well as the earth are filled with the good will of Him that dwelt in the bush. The perfect blood of atonement secures this forever.

Whoever will listen will hear the speaking Heaven. This is definitely not the hour when men take kindly to an exhortation to *listen,* for listening is not today a part of popular religion. We are at the opposite end of the pole from there. Religion has accepted the monstrous heresy that noise, size, activity and bluster make a man dear to God. But we may take heart. To a people caught in the tempest of the last great conflict God says, "Be still, and know that I am God," and still He says it, as if He means to tell us that our strength and safety lie not in noise but in silence.

It is important that we get still to wait on God. And it is best that we get alone, preferably with our Bible outspread before us. Then if we will we may draw near to God and begin to hear Him speak to us in our hearts. I think for the average person the progression will be something like this: First a sound as of a Presence walking in the garden. Then a voice, more intelligible, but still far from clear. Then the happy moment when the Spirit begins to illuminate the Scriptures, and that which had been only a sound, or at best a voice, now becomes an intelligible word, warm and intimate and clear as the word of a dear friend. Then will come life and light, and best of all, ability to see and rest in and embrace Jesus Christ as Saviour and Lord and All.

The Bible will never be a living Book to us until we are convinced that God is articulate in His universe. To jump from a dead, impersonal world to a dogmatic Bible is too much for most people. They may admit that they *should* accept the Bible as the Word of God, and they may try to think of it as such, but they find it impossible to believe that the words there on the page are actually for them. A man may *say*, "These words are addressed to me," and yet in his heart not feel and know that they are. He is the victim of a divided psychology. He tries to think of God as mute everywhere else and vocal only in a book.

I believe that much of our religious unbelief is due to a wrong conception of and a wrong feeling for the Scriptures of Truth. A silent God suddenly began to speak in a book and when the book was finished lapsed back into silence again forever. Now we read the book as the record of what God said when He was for a brief time in a speaking mood. With notions like that in our heads how can we believe? The facts are that God is not silent, has never been silent. It is the nature of God to speak. The second Person of the Holy Trinity is called the *Word*. The Bible is the inevitable outcome of God's continuous speech. It is the infallible declaration of His mind—for us put into our familiar human words.

I think a new world will arise out of the religious mists when we approach our Bible with the idea that it is not only a book which was once spoken, but a book which is *now speaking*. The prophets habitually said, "Thus *saith* the Lord." They meant their hearers to understand that God's speaking is in the continuous present. We may use the past tense properly to indicate that at a certain time a certain word of God was spoken, but a word of God once spoken continues to be spoken, as a child once born continues to be alive, or a world once created continues to exist. And those are but imperfect illustrations, for children die and worlds burn out, but the Word of our God endureth forever.

If you would follow on to know the Lord, come at once to the open Bible expecting it to speak to you. Do not come with the notion that it is a *thing* which you may push around at your convenience. It is more than a thing, it is a voice, a word, the very Word of the living God.

Lord, teach me to listen. The times are noisy and my ears are weary with the thousand raucous sounds which continuously assault them. Give me the spirit of the boy Samuel when he said to Thee, "Speak, for thy servant heareth." Let me hear Thee speaking in my heart. Let me get used to the sound of Thy Voice, that its tones may be familiar when the sounds of earth die away and the only sound will be the music of Thy speaking Voice. Amen.

3

Meekness and Rest

*Blessed are the meek: for they shall
inherit the earth.*

Matt. 5:5

A fairly accurate description of the human race might
be furnished one unacquainted with it by taking the
Beatitudes, turning them wrong side out and saying,
"Here is your human race." For the exact opposite of the
virtues in the Beatitudes are the very qualities which
distinguish human life and conduct.

In the world of men we find nothing approaching the
virtues of which Jesus spoke in the opening words of the
famous Sermon on the Mount. Instead of poverty of spirit
we find the rankest kind of pride; instead of mourners
we find pleasure seekers; instead of meekness, arrogance;
instead of hunger after righteousness we hear men saying, "I am rich and increased with goods and have need
of nothing"; instead of mercy we find cruelty; instead of
purity of heart, corrupt imaginings; instead of peace-
makers we find men quarrelsome and resentful; instead
of rejoicing in mistreatment we find them fighting back
with every weapon at their command.

Of this kind of moral stuff civilized society is composed.
The atmosphere is charged with it; we breathe it with every breath and drink it with our mother's milk. Culture
and education refine these things slightly but leave them
basically untouched. A whole world of literature has been
created to justify this kind of life as the only normal one.
And this is the more to be wondered at, seeing that these
are the evils which make life the bitter struggle it is for all

of us. All our heartaches and a great many of our physical ills spring directly out of our sins. Pride, arrogance, resentfulness, evil imaginings, malice, greed: these are the sources of more human pain than all the diseases that ever afflicted mortal flesh.

Into a world like this the sound of Jesus' words comes wonderful and strange, a visitation from above. It is well that He spoke, for no one else could have done it as well; and it is good that we listen. His words are the essence of truth. He is not offering an opinion; Jesus never uttered opinions. He never guessed; He knew, and He knows. His words are not as Solomon's were, the sum of sound wisdom or the results of keen observation. He spoke out of the fulness of His Godhead, and His words are very Truth itself. He is the only one who could say "blessed" with complete authority, for He is the Blessed One come from the world above to confer blessedness upon mankind. And His words were supported by deeds mightier than any performed on this earth by any other man. It is wisdom for us to listen.

As was often so with Jesus, He used this word "meek" in a brief crisp sentence, and not till some time later did He go on to explain it. In the same book of Matthew He tells us more about it and applies it to our lives. "Come unto me, all ye that labour and are heavy laden, and I will give you rest. Take my yoke upon you, and learn of me; for I am meek and lowly in heart: and ye shall find rest unto your souls. For my yoke is easy, and my burden is light." Here we have two things standing in contrast to each other, a burden and a rest. The burden is not a local one, peculiar to those first hearers, but one which is borne by the whole human race. It consists not of political oppression or poverty or hard work. It is far deeper than that. It is felt by the rich as well as the poor for it is something from which wealth and idleness can never deliver us.

The burden borne by mankind is a heavy and a crushing thing. The word Jesus used means a load carried or toil borne to the point of exhaustion. Rest is simply release from that burden. It is not something we do, it is what comes to us when we cease to do. His own meekness, that is the rest.

Let us examine our burden. It is altogether an interior one. It attacks the heart and the mind and reaches the body only from within. First, there is the burden of *pride*. The labor of self-love is a heavy one indeed. Think for yourself whether much of your sorrow has not arisen from someone speaking slightingly of you. As long as you set yourself up as a little god to which you must be loyal there will be those who will delight to offer affront to your idol. How then can you hope to have inward peace? The heart's fierce effort to protect itself from every slight, to shield its touchy honor from the bad opinion of friend and enemy, will never let the mind have rest. Continue this fight through the years and the burden will become intolerable. Yet the sons of earth are carrying this burden continually, challenging every word spoken against them, cringing under every criticism, smarting under each fancied slight, tossing sleepless if another is preferred before them.

Such a burden as this is not necessary to bear. Jesus calls us to His rest, and meekness is His method. The meek man cares not at all who is greater than he, for he has long ago decided that the esteem of the world is not worth the effort. He develops toward himself a kindly sense of humor and learns to say, "Oh, so you have been overlooked? They have placed someone else before you? They have whispered that you are pretty small stuff after all? And now you feel hurt because the world is saying about you the very things you have been saying about yourself? Only yesterday you were telling God that you were nothing, a mere worm of the dust. Where is your consistency? Come on, humble yourself, and cease to care what men think."

The meek man is not a human mouse afflicted with a sense of his own inferiority. Rather he may be in his moral life as bold as a lion and as strong as Samson; but he has stopped being fooled about himself. He has accepted God's estimate of his own life. He knows he is as weak and helpless as God has declared him to be, but paradoxically, he knows at the same time that he is in the sight of God of more importance than angels. In himself, nothing; in God, everything. That is his motto. He knows well that the world will never see him as God sees him and he has stopped caring. He rests perfectly content to allow God to place His own values. He will be patient to wait for the day when everything will get its own price tag and real worth will come into its own. Then the righteous shall shine forth in the Kingdom of their Father. He is willing to wait for that day.

In the meantime he will have attained a place of soul rest. As he walks on in meekness he will be happy to let God defend him. The old struggle to defend himself is over. He has found the peace which meekness brings.

Then also he will get deliverance from the burden of *pretense.* By this I mean not hypocrisy, but the common human desire to put the best foot forward and hide from the world our real inward poverty. For sin has played many evil tricks upon us, and one has been the infusing into us a false sense of shame. There is hardly a man or woman who dares to be just what he or she is without doctoring up the impression. The fear of being found out gnaws like rodents within their hearts. The man of culture is haunted by the fear that he will some day come upon a man more cultured than himself. The learned man fears to meet a man more learned than he. The rich man sweats under the fear that his clothes or his car or his house will sometime be made to look cheap by comparison with those of another rich man. So-called "society" runs by a motivation not higher than this, and the poorer classes on their level are little better.

Let no one smile this off. These burdens are real, and little by little they kill the victims of this evil and unnatural way of life. And the psychology created by years of this kind of thing makes true meekness seem as unreal as a dream, as aloof as a star. To all the victims of the gnawing disease Jesus says, "Ye must become as little children." For little children do not compare; they receive direct enjoyment from what they have without relating it to something else or someone else. Only as they get older and sin begins to stir within their hearts do jealousy and envy appear. Then they are unable to enjoy what they have if someone else has something larger or better. At that early age, the galling burden comes down upon their tender souls, and it never leaves them till Jesus sets them free.

Another source of burden is *artificiality*. I am sure that most people live in secret fear that some day they will be careless and by chance an enemy or friend will be allowed to peep into their poor empty souls. So they are never relaxed. Bright people are tense and alert in fear that they may be trapped into saying something common or stupid. Traveled people are afraid that they may meet some Marco Polo who is able to describe some remote place where they have never been.

This unnatural condition is part of our sad heritage of sin, but in our day it is aggravated by our whole way of life. Advertising is largely based upon this habit of pretense. "Courses" are offered in this or that field of human learning frankly appealing to the victim's desire to shine at a party. Books are sold, clothes and cosmetics are peddled, by playing continually upon this desire to appear what we are not. Artificiality is one curse that will drop away the moment we kneel at Jesus' feet and surrender ourselves to His meekness. Then we will not care what people think of us so long as God is pleased. Then *what we are* will be everything; what we appear will take its place far down the scale of interest for us. Apart from sin we have nothing of which to be ashamed. Only an evil desire to shine makes us want to appear other than we are.

The heart of the world is breaking under this load of pride and pretense. There is no release from our burden apart from the meekness of Christ. Good, keen reasoning may help slightly, but so strong is this vice that if we push it down one place it will come up somewhere else. To men and women everywhere Jesus says, "Come unto me, and I will give you rest." The rest He offers is the rest of meekness, the blessed relief which comes when we accept ourselves for what we are and cease to pretend. It will take some courage at first, but the needed grace will come as we learn that we are sharing this new and easy yoke with the strong Son of God Himself. He calls it "my yoke," and He walks at one end while we walk at the other.

Lord, make me childlike. Deliver me from the urge to compete with another for place or prestige or position. I would be simple and artless as a little child. Deliver me from pose and pretense. Forgive me for thinking of myself. Help me to forget myself and find my true peace in beholding Thee. That Thou mayest answer this prayer, I humble myself before Thee. Lay upon me Thy easy yoke of self-forgetfulness that through it I may find rest. Amen.

4

Born After Midnight

Among revival-minded Christians I have heard the saying, "Revivals are born after midnight."

This is one of those proverbs which, while not quite literally true, yet points to something very true.

If we understand the saying to mean that God does not hear our prayer for revival made in the daytime, it is of course not true. If we take it to mean that prayer offered when we are tired and worn-out has greater power than prayer made when we are rested and fresh, again it is not true. God would need to be very austere indeed to require us to turn our prayer into penance, or to enjoy seeing us punish ourselves by intercession. Traces of such ascetical notions are still found among some gospel Christians, and while these brethren are to be commended for their zeal, they are not to be excused for unconsciously attributing to God a streak of sadism unworthy of fallen men.

Yet there is considerable truth in the idea that revivals are born after midnight, for revivals (or any other spiritual gifts and graces) come only to those who want them badly enough. It may be said without qualification that every man is as holy and as full of the Spirit as he wants to be. He may not be as full as he wishes he were, but he is most certainly as full as he wants to be.

Our Lord placed this beyond dispute when He said, "Blessed are they which do hunger and thirst after righteousness: for they shall be filled." Hunger and thirst are physical sensations which, in their acute stages, may become real pain. It has been the experience of countless seekers after God that when their desires became a pain they were suddenly and wonderfully filled. The problem is not to persuade God to fill us, but to want God sufficiently to permit Him to do so. The average Christian is so cold and so contented with His wretched condition that there is no vacuum of desire into which the blessed Spirit can rush in satisfying fullness.

Occasionally there will appear on the religious scene a man whose unsatisfied spiritual longings become so big and important in his life that they crowd out every other interest. Such a man refuses to be content with the safe and conventional prayers of the frost-bound brethren who "lead in prayer" week after week and year after year in the local assemblies. His yearnings carry him away and often make something of a nuisance out of him. His puzzled fellow Christians shake their heads and look knowingly at each other, but like the blind man who cried after his sight and was rebuked by the disciples, he "cries the more a great deal." And if he has not yet met the conditions or there is something hindering the answer to his prayer, he may pray on into the late hours. Not the hour of night but the state of his heart decides the time of his visitation. For him it may well be that revival comes after midnight.

It is very important, however, that we understand that long prayer vigils, or even strong crying and tears, are not in themselves meritorious acts. Every blessing flows out of the goodness of God as from a fountain. Even those rewards for good works about which certain teachers talk so fulsomely, and which they always set in sharp contrast to the benefits received by grace alone, are at bottom as certainly of grace as is the forgiveness of sin itself. The holiest apostle can claim no more than that he is an unprofitable servant. The very angels exist out of the pure goodness of God. No creature can "earn" anything in the usual meaning of the word. All things are by and of the sovereign goodness of God.

Lady Julian summed it up quaintly when she wrote, "It is more honor to God, and more very delight, that we faithfully pray to Himself of His goodness and cleave thereunto by His grace, and with true understanding, and steadfast by love, than if we took all the means that heart can think. For if we took all those means it is too little, and not full honor to God. But in His goodness is all the whole, and there faileth right nought . . . For the goodness of God is the highest prayer, and it cometh down to the lowest part of our need."

Yet for all God's good will toward us, He is unable to grant us our heart's desires till all our desires have been reduced to one. When we have dealt with our carnal ambitions; when we have trodden upon the lion and adder of the flesh, have trampled the dragon of self-love under our feet and have truly reckoned ourselves to have died unto sin, then and only then can God raise us to newness of life and fill us with His blessed Holy Spirit.

It is easy to learn the doctrine of personal revival and victorious living; it is quite another thing to take our cross and plod on to the dark and bitter hill of self-renunciation. Here many are called and few are chosen. For every one that actually crosses over into the Promised Land there are many who stand for a while and look longingly across the river and then turn sadly back to the comparative safety of the sandy wastes of the old life.

No, there is no merit in late hour prayers, but it requires a serious mind and a determined heart to pray past the ordinary into the unusual. Most Christians never do. And it is more than possible that the rare soul who presses on into the unusual experience reaches there after midnight.

5

The Erotic vs. the Spiritual

The period in which we now live may well go down in history as the Erotic Age. Sex love has been elevated into a cult. Eros has more worshipers among civilized men today than any other god. For millions the erotic has completely displaced the spiritual.

How the world got into this state is not difficult to trace. Contributing factors are the phonograph and radio, which can spread a love song from coast to coast within a matter of days; the motion picture and television, which enable a whole population to feast their eyes on sensuous women and amorous young men locked in passionate embrace (and this in the living rooms of "Christian" homes and before the eyes of innocent children!); shorter working hours and a multiplicity of mechanical gadgets with the resultant increased leisure for everyone. Add to these the scores of shrewdly contrived advertising campaigns which make sex the not too slyly concealed bait to attract buyers for almost every imaginable product; the degraded columnists who have consecrated their lives to the task of the publicizing of soft, slinky nobodies with the faces of angels and the morals of alley cats; conscienceless novelists who win a doubtful fame and grow rich at the inglorious chore of dredging up literary putridities from the sewers of their souls to provide entertainment for the masses. These tell us something about how Eros has achieved his triumph over the civilized world.

Now if this god would let us Christians alone, I for one would let his cult alone. The whole spongy, fetid mess will sink some day under its own weight and become excellent fuel for the fires of hell, a just recompense which is meet, and it becomes us to feel compassion for those who have been caught in its tragic collapse. Tears and silence might be better than words if things were slightly otherwise than they are. But the cult of Eros is seriously affecting the Church. The pure religion of Christ that flows like a crystal river from the heart of God is being polluted by the unclean waters that trickle from behind the altars of abomination that appear on every high hill and under every green tree from New York to Los Angeles.

The influence of the erotic spirit is felt almost everywhere in evangelical circles. Much of the singing in certain types of meetings has in it more of romance than it has of the Holy Ghost. Both words and music are designed to rouse the libidinous. Christ is courted with a familiarity that reveals a total ignorance of who He is. It is not the reverent intimacy of the adoring saint but the impudent familiarity of the carnal lover.

Religious fiction also makes use of sex to interest the reading public, the paper-thin excuse being that if romance and religion are woven into a story the average person who would not read a purely religious book will read the story and thus be exposed to the gospel. Leaving aside the fact that most modern religious novelists are home-talent amateurs, scarcely one of whom is capable of writing a single line of even fair literature, the whole concept behind the religio-romantic novel is unsound. The libidinous impulses and the sweet, deep movings of the Holy Spirit are diametrically opposed to each other. The notion that Eros can be made to serve as an assistant of the Lord of glory is outrageous. The "Christian" film that seeks to draw customers by picturing amorous love scenes in its advertising is completely false to the religion of Christ. Only the spiritually blind will be taken in by it.

The current vogue of physical beauty and sparkling personalities in religious promotion is a further manifestation of the influence of the romantic spirit in the Church. The rhythmic sway, the synthetic smile and the too, too cheerful voice betray the religious worldling. He has learned his technique from the TV screen but not learned it well enough to succeed in the professional field, so he brings his inept production to the holy place and peddles it to the ailing and undersized Christians who are looking for something to amuse them while staying within the bounds of the current religious mores.

If my language should seem severe, let it be remembered that it is not directed at any individual. Toward the lost world of men I feel only a great compassion and a desire that all should come to repentance. For the Christians whose vigorous but mistaken leadership has wooed the modern church from the altar of Jehovah to the altars of error I feel genuine love and sympathy. I want to be the last to injure them and the first to forgive them, remembering my past sins and my need for mercy, as well as my own weakness and natural bent toward sin and error. Balaam's ass was used of God to rebuke a prophet. It would seem from this that God does not require perfection in the instrument He uses to warn and exhort His people.

When God's sheep are in danger, the shepherd must not gaze at the stars and meditate on "inspirational" themes. He is morally obliged to grab his weapon and run to their defense. When the circumstances call for it, love can use the sword, though by her nature she would rather bind up the broken heart and minister to the wounded. It is time for the prophet and the seer to make themselves heard and felt again. For the last three decades timidity disguised as humility has crouched in her corner while the spiritual quality of evangelical Christianity has become progressively worse year by year. *How long, O Lord, how long?*

6

To Be Right, We Must Think Right

What we think about when we are free to think about what we will—that is what we are or will soon become.

The Bible has a great deal to say about our thoughts; current evangelicalism has practically nothing to say about them. The reason the Bible says so much is that our thoughts are so vitally important to us; the reason evangelicalism says so little is that we are over-reacting from the "thought" cults, such as New Thought, Unity, Christian Science and their like. These cults make our thoughts to be very nearly everything and we counter by making them very nearly nothing. Both positions are wrong.

Our voluntary thoughts not only reveal what we are, they predict what we will become. Except for that conduct which springs from our basic natural instincts, all conscious behavior is preceded by and arises out of our thoughts. The will can become a servant of the thoughts, and to a large degree even our emotions follow our thinking. "The more I think about it the madder I get" is the way the average man states it, and in so doing not only reports accurately on his own mental processes but pays as well an unconscious tribute to the power of thought. Thinking stirs feeling and feeling triggers action. That is the way we are made and we may as well accept it.

The Psalms and Prophets contain numerous references to the power of right thinking to raise religious feeling and incite to right conduct. "I thought on my ways, and turned my feet unto thy testimonies." "While I was musing the fire burned: then spake I with my tongue." Over and over the Old Testament writers exhort us to get quiet and think about high and holy things as a preliminary to amendment of life or a good deed or a courageous act.

The Old Testament is not alone in its respect for the God-given power of human thought. Christ taught that men defile themselves by evil thinking and even went so far as to equate a thought with an act: "Whosoever looketh on a woman to lust after her hath committed adultery with her already in his heart." Paul recited a list of shining virtues and commanded, "Think on these things."

These quotations are but four out of hundreds that could be cited from the Scriptures. Thinking about God and holy things creates a moral climate favorable to the growth of faith and love and humility and reverence. We cannot by thinking regenerate our hearts, nor take our sins away nor change the leopard's spots. Neither can we by thinking add one cubit to our stature or make evil good or darkness light. So to teach is to misrepresent a scriptural truth and to use it to our own undoing. But we can by Spirit-inspired thinking help to make our minds pure sanctuaries in which God will be pleased to dwell.

I referred in a previous paragraph to "our voluntary thoughts" and I used the words advisedly. In our journey through this evil and hostile world, many thoughts will be forced upon us which we do not like and for which we have no moral sympathy. The necessity to make a living may compel us for days on end to entertain thoughts in no sense elevating. Ordinary awareness of the doings of our fellow men will bring thoughts repugnant to our Christian soul. These need affect us but little. For them we are not responsible and they may pass through our minds like a bird through the air, without leaving a trace. They have no lasting effect upon us because they are not our own. They are unwelcome intruders for which we have no love and which we get rid of as quickly as possible.

Anyone who wishes to check on his true spiritual condition may do so by noting what his voluntary thoughts have been over the last hours or days. What has he thought about when free to think of what he pleased? Toward what has his inner heart turned when it was free to turn where it would? When the bird of thought was let go, did it fly out like the raven to settle upon floating carcasses or did it like the dove circle and return again to the ark of God? Such a test is easy to run, and if we are honest with ourselves we can discover not only what we are but what we are going to become. We'll soon be the sum of our voluntary thoughts.

While our thoughts stir our feelings, and thus strongly influence our wills, it is yet true that the will can be and should be master of our thoughts. Every normal person can determine what he will think about. Of course the troubled or tempted man may find his thoughts somewhat difficult to control and even while he is concentrating upon a worthy object, wild and fugitive thoughts may play over his mind like heat lightning on a summer evening. These are likely to be more bothersome than harmful and in the long run do not make much difference one way or another.

The best way to control our thoughts is to offer the mind to God in complete surrender. The Holy Spirit will accept it and take control of it immediately. Then it will be relatively easy to think on spiritual things, especially if we train our thought by long periods of daily prayer. Long practice in the art of mental prayer (that is, talking to God inwardly as we work or travel) will help to form the habit of holy thought.

7

Faith Dares to Fail

In this world men are judged by their ability to do.

They are rated according to the distance they have come up the hill of achievement. At the bottom is utter failure; at the top complete success, and between these two extremes the majority of civilized men sweat and struggle from youth to old age.

A few give up, slide to the bottom and become inhabitants of Skid Row. There, with ambition gone and will broken, they subsist on handouts till nature forecloses on them and death takes them away.

At the top are the few who by a combination of talent, hard work and good fortune manage to reach the peak and all the luxury, fame, and power that are found there.

But in all of this there is no happiness. The effort to succeed puts too much strain on the nerves. Excessive preoccupation with the struggle to win narrows the mind, hardens the heart, and shuts out a thousand bright visions which might be enjoyed if there were only leisure to notice them.

The man who reaches the pinnacle is seldom happy for very long. He soon becomes eaten by fears that he may slip back a peg and be forced to surrender his place to another. Examples of this are found in the feverish way the TV star watches his rating and the politician his mail.

Let an elected official learn that a poll shows him to be two per cent less popular in August than he was in March and he begins to sweat like a man on his way to prison. The ball player lives by his averages, the businessman by his rising graph and the concert star by his applause meter. It is not uncommon for a challenger in the ring to weep openly when he fails to knock out the champion. To be second best leaves him completely disconsolate; he must be first to be happy.

This mania to succeed is a good thing perverted. The desire to fulfill the purpose for which we were created is of course a gift from God, but sin has twisted this impulse about and turned it into a selfish lust for first place and top honors. By this lust the whole world of mankind is driven as by a demon, and there is no escape.

When we come to Christ we enter a different world. The New Testament introduces us to a spiritual philosophy infinitely higher than and altogether contrary to that which motivates the world. According to the teaching of Christ the poor in spirit are blessed; the meek inherit the earth; the first are last and the last first; the greatest man is the one that best serves others; the one who loses everything is the only one that will have everything at last; the successful man of the world will see his hoarded treasures swept away by the tempest of judgment; the righteous beggar goes to Abraham's bosom and the rich man burns in the fires of hell.

Our Lord died an apparent failure, discredited by the leaders of established religion, rejected by society and forsaken by His friends. The man who ordered Him to the cross was the successful statesman whose hand the ambitious hack politician kissed. It took the resurrection to demonstrate how gloriously Christ had triumphed and how tragically the governor had failed.

Yet today the professed church seems to have learned nothing. We are still seeing as men see and judging after the manner of man's judgment. How much eager-beaver religious work is done out of a carnal desire to make good? How many hours of prayer are wasted beseeching God to bless projects that are geared to the glorification of little men? How much sacred money is poured out upon men who, in spite of their tear-in-the-voice appeals, nevertheless seek only to make a fair show in the flesh?

The true Christian should turn away from all this. Especially should ministers of the gospel search their own hearts and look deep into their inner motives. No man is worthy to succeed until he is willing to fail. No man is morally worthy of success in religious activities until he is willing that the honor of succeeding should go to another if God so wills.

God may allow His servant to succeed when He has disciplined him to a point where he does not need to succeed to be happy. The man who is elated by success and cast down by failure is still a carnal man. At best his fruit will have a worm in it.

God will allow His servant to succeed when he has learned that success does not make him dearer to God nor more valuable in the total scheme of things. We cannot buy God's favor with crowds or converts or new missionaries sent out or Bibles distributed. All these things can be accomplished without the help of the Holy Spirit. A good personality and a shrewd knowledge of human nature is all that any man needs to be a success in religious circles today.

Our great honor lies in being just what Jesus was and is. To be accepted by those who accept Him, rejected by all who reject Him, loved by those who love Him and hated by everyone that hates Him. What greater glory could come to any man?

We can afford to follow Him to failure. Faith dares to fail. The resurrection and the judgment will demonstrate before all worlds who won and who lost. We can wait.

8

The Value of a Sanctified Imagination

Like every other power belonging to us, the imagination may be either a blessing or a curse, depending altogether upon how it is used and how well it is disciplined.

We all have to some degree the power to imagine. This gift enables us to see meanings in material objects, to observe similarities between things which at first appear wholly unlike each other. It permits us to know that which the senses can never tell us, for by it we are able to see through sense impressions to the reality that lies behind things.

Every advance made by mankind in any field began as an idea to which nothing for the time corresponded. The mind of the inventor simply took bits of familiar ideas and made out of them something which was not only wholly unfamiliar but which up to that time was altogether non-existent. Thus we "create" things and by so doing prove ourselves to have been made in the image of the Creator. That fallen man has often used his creative powers in the service of evil does not invalidate our argument. Any talent may be used for evil as well as for good, but every talent comes from God nevertheless.

That the imagination is of great value in the service of God may be denied by some persons who have erroneously confused the word "imaginative" with the word "imaginary."

The gospel of Jesus Christ has no truck with things

imaginary. The most realistic book in the world is the Bible. God is real, men are real and so is sin and so are death and hell, toward which sin inevitably leads. The presence of God is not imaginary, neither is prayer the indulgence of a delightful fancy. The objects that engage the praying man's attention, while not material, are nevertheless completely real; more certainly real, it will at last be admitted, than any earthly object.

The value of the cleansed imagination in the sphere of religion lies in its power to perceive in natural things shadows of things spiritual. It enables the reverent man to

> See the world in a grain of sand
> And eternity in an hour.

The weakness of the Pharisee in days of old was his lack of imagination, or what amounted to the same thing, his refusal to let it enter the field of religion. He saw the text with its carefully guarded theological definition and he saw nothing beyond.

> A primrose by the river's brim
> A yellow primrose was to him,
> And it was nothing more.

When Christ came with His blazing spiritual penetration and His fine moral sensitivity, He appeared to the Pharisee to be a devotee of another kind of religion, which indeed He was if the world had only understood. He could see the soul of the text while the Pharisee could see only the body, and he could always prove Christ wrong by an appeal to the letter of the law or to an interpretation hallowed by tradition. The breach between them was too great to permit them to coexist; so the Pharisee, who was in a position to do it, had the young Seer put to death. So it has always been, and so I suppose it will always be till the earth is filled with the knowledge of the Lord as the waters cover the sea.

The imagination, since it is a faculty of the natural mind, must necessarily suffer both from its intrinsic limitations and from an inherent bent toward evil. While the word as found in the King James Bible usually means not imagination at all, but merely the reasonings of sinful men, I yet do not write to excuse the unsanctified imagination. I well know that from such have flowed as from a polluted fountain streams of evil ideas which have throughout the years led to lawless and destructive conduct on the part of men.

A purified and Spirit-controlled imagination is, however, quite another thing, and it is this I have in mind here. I long to see the imagination released from its prison and given to its proper place among the sons of the new creation. What I am trying to describe here is the sacred gift of seeing, the ability to peer beyond the veil and gaze with astonished wonder upon the beauties and mysteries of things holy and eternal.

The stodgy pedestrian mind does no credit to Christianity. Let it dominate the church long enough and it will force her to take one of two directions: either toward liberalism, where she will find relief in a false freedom, or toward the world, where she will find an enjoyable but fatal pleasure.

But I wonder whether this is not all included in the words of our Lord as recorded in the Gospel of John: "Howbeit when he, the Spirit of truth, is come, he will guide you into all truth: for he shall not speak of himself; but whatsoever he shall hear, that shall he speak: and he will shew you things to come. He shall glorify me: for he shall receive of mine, and shall shew it unto you" (16:13, 14).

To possess a Spirit-indwelt mind is the Christian's privilege under grace, and this embraces all I have been trying to say here.

9

Nearness Is Likeness

One serious and often distressing problem for many Christians is their feeling that God is far from them, or that they are far from God, which is the same thing.

It is hard to rejoice in the Lord when we are suffering from this sense of remoteness. It is like trying to have a warm, bright summer without the sun. The chief trouble here is of course not intellectual and cannot be cured by intellectual means; yet truth must enter the mind before it can enter the heart, so let us reason together about this. In spiritual matters we think correctly only when we boldly rule out the concept of space. God is spirit, and spirit dwells not in space. Space has to do with matter and spirit is independent of it. By the concept of space we account for the relation of material bodies to each other.

We should never think of God as being spatially near or remote, for He is not here or there but carries here and there in His heart. Space is not infinite, as some have thought; only God is infinite and in His infinitude He swallows up all space. "Do not I fill heaven and earth? saith the Lord." He fills heaven and earth as the ocean fills the bucket that is submerged in it, and as the ocean surrounds the bucket so does God in the universe He fills. "The heaven of heavens cannot contain thee." God is not contained: He contains.

As earthborn creatures we naturally tend to think by earthly analogies. "He that is of the earth is earthly, and speaketh of the earth." God created us living souls and gave us bodies through which we can experience the world around us and communicate with one another. When man fell through sin he began to think of himself as having a soul instead of being one. It makes a lot of difference whether a man believes that he is a body having a soul or a soul having a body.

The soul is inward and hidden, while the body is always present to the senses; consequently we tend to be body-conscious, and the concept of near and remote, which attaches to material things, seems quite natural to us. But it is valid only when it applies to moral creatures. When we try to apply it to God it no longer retains its validity.

Yet when we speak of men being "far" from God we speak truly. The Lord said of Israel, "Their heart is far from me," and there we have the definition of far and near in our relation to God. The words refer not to physical distance, but to likeness.

That God is equally near to all parts of His universe is plainly taught in the Scriptures (Ps. 139:1-18), yet some beings experience His nearness and others do not, depending upon their moral likeness to Him. It is dissimilarity that creates the sense of remoteness between creatures and between men and God.

Two creatures may be so close physically that they touch, yet because of dissimilarity of nature be millions of miles apart. An angel and an ape might conceivably be in the same room, but the radical difference between their natures would make communion impossible. They would be "far" from each other in fact.

For the moral unlikeness between man and God the Bible has a word, alienation, and the Holy Spirit presents a frightful picture of this alienation as it works itself out in human character. Fallen human nature is precisely opposite to the nature of God as revealed in Jesus Christ. Because there is no moral likeness there is no communion, hence the sense of physical distance, the feeling that God is far away in space. This erroneous notion discourages prayer and prevents many a sinner from believing unto life.

Paul encouraged the Athenians by reminding them that God was not far from any one of them, that it was He in whom they lived and moved and had their being. Yet men think of Him as farther away than the farthest star. The truth is that He is nearer to us than we are to ourselves.

But how can the conscious sinner bridge the mighty gulf that separates him from God in living experience? The answer is that he cannot, but the glory of the Christian message is that Christ did. Through the blood of His cross He made peace that He might reconcile all things unto Himself. "And you, that were sometime alienated and enemies in your mind by wicked works, yet now hath he reconciled in the body of his flesh through death, to present you holy and unblameable and unreproveable in his sight" (Col. 1:21, 22).

The new birth makes us partakers of the divine nature. There the work of undoing the dissimilarity between us and God begins. From there it progresses by the sanctifying operation of the Holy Spirit till God is satisfied.

That is the theology of it, but as I said, even the regenerated soul may sometimes suffer from the feeling that God is far from Him. What then should he do?

First, the trouble may be no more than a temporary break in God-conscious communion due to any one of half a hundred causes. The cure is faith. Trust God in the dark till the light returns.

Second, should the sense of remoteness persist in spite of prayer and what you believe is faith, look to your inner life for evidences of wrong attitudes, evil thoughts or dispositional flaws. These are unlike God and create a psychological gulf between you and Him. Put away the evil from you, believe, and the sense of nearness will be restored. God was never away in the first place.

10
Why We Are Lukewarm About Christ's Return

Shortly after the close of the first World War, I heard a great Southern preacher say that he feared the intense interest in prophecy current at that time would result in a dying out of the blessed hope when events had proved the excited interpreters wrong.

The man was a prophet, or at least a remarkably shrewd student of human nature, for exactly what he predicted has come to pass. The hope of Christ's coming is today all but dead among evangelicals.

I do not mean that Bible Christians have given up the doctrine of the second advent. By no means. There has been, as every informed person knows, an adjustment among some of the lesser tenets of our prophetic credo, but the vast majority of evangelicals continue to hold to the belief that Jesus Christ will sometime actually come back to the earth in person. The ultimate triumph of Christ is accepted as one of the unshakable doctrines of Holy Scripture.

It is true that in some quarters the prophecies of the Bible are occasionally expounded. This is especially so among Hebrew Christians who, for reasons well understood, seem to feel closer to the prophets of the Old Testament than do Gentile believers. Their love for their own people naturally leads them to grasp at every hope of the conversion and ultimate restoration of Israel. To many of them the return of Christ represents a quick and happy solution of the "Jewish problem." The long centuries of wandering will end when He comes and God will at that time "restore again the kingdom to Israel." We dare not allow our deep love for our Hebrew Christian brethren to blind us to the obvious political implications of this aspect of their Messianic hope. We do not blame them for this. We merely call attention to it.

Yet the return of Christ as a blessed hope is, as I have said, all but dead among us. The truth touching the second advent, where it is presented today, is for the most part either academic or political. The joyful personal element is altogether missing. Where are they who

> Yearn for the sign, O Christ, of Thy fulfilling,
> Faint for the flaming of Thine advent feet?

The longing to see Christ that burned in the breasts of those first Christians seems to have burned itself out. All we have left are the ashes. It is precisely the "yearning" and the "fainting" for the return of Christ that has distinguished the personal hope from the theological one. Mere acquaintance with correct doctrine is a poor substitute for Christ and familiarity with New Testament eschatology will never take the place of a love-inflamed desire to look on His face.

If the tender yearning is gone from the advent hope today, there must be a reason for it; and I think I know what it is, or what they are, for there are a number of them. One is simply that popular fundamentalist theology has emphasized the utility of the cross rather than the beauty of the One who died on it. The saved man's relation to Christ has been made contractual instead of personal. The "work" of Christ has been stressed until it has eclipsed the person of Christ. Substitution has been allowed to supersede identification. What He did for me seems to be more important than what He is to me. Redemption is seen as an across-the-counter transaction which we "accept," and the whole thing lacks emotional content. We must love someone very much to stay awake and long for his coming, and that may explain the absence of power in the advent hope even among those who still believe in it.

Another reason for the absence of real yearning for Christ's return is that Christians are so comfortable in this world that they have little desire to leave it. For those leaders who set the pace of religion and determine its content and quality, Christianity has become of late remarkably lucrative. The streets of gold do not have too great an appeal for those who find it so easy to pile up gold and silver in the service of the Lord here on earth. We all want to reserve the hope of heaven as a kind of insurance against the day of death, but as long as we are healthy and comfortable, why change a familiar good for something about which we actually know very little? So reasons the carnal mind, and so subtly that we are scarcely aware of it.

Again, in these times religion has become jolly good fun right here in this present world, and what's the hurry about heaven anyway? Christianity, contrary to what some had thought, is another and higher form of entertainment. Christ has done all the suffering. He has shed all the tears and carried all the crosses; we have but to enjoy the benefits of His heartbreak in the form of religious pleasures modeled after the world but carried on in the name of Jesus. So say the same people who claim to believe in Christ's second coming.

History reveals that times of suffering for the Church have also been times of looking upward. Tribulation has always sobered God's people and encouraged them to look for and yearn after the return of their Lord. Our present preoccupation with this world may be a warning of bitter days to come. God will wean us from the earth some way—the easy way if possible, the hard way if necessary. It is up to us.

11

God Tells the Man Who Cares

The Bible was written in tears and to tears it will yield its best treasures. God has nothing to say to the frivolous man.

It was to Moses, a trembling man, that God spoke on the mount, and that same man later saved the nation when he threw himself before God with the offer to have himself blotted out of God's book for Israel's sake. Daniel's long season of fasting and prayer brought Gabriel from heaven to tell him the secret of the centuries. When the beloved John wept much because no one could be found worthy to open the seven-sealed book, one of the elders comforted him with the joyous news that the Lion of the tribe of Judah had prevailed.

The psalmists often wrote in tears, the prophets could hardly conceal their heavyheartedness, and the apostle Paul in his otherwise joyous epistle to the Philippians broke into tears when he thought of the many who were enemies of the cross of Christ and whose end was destruction. Those Christian leaders who shook the world were one and all men of sorrows whose witness to mankind welled out of heavy hearts: There is no power in tears per se, but tears and power ever lie close together in the Church of the First-born.

It is not a reassuring thought that the writings of the grief-stricken prophets are often pored over by persons whose interests are merely curious and who never shed one tear for the woes of the world. They have a prying inquisitiveness about the schedule of future events, forgetting that the whole purpose of Bible prophecy is to prepare us morally and spiritually for the time to come.

The doctrine of Christ's return has fallen into neglect, on the North American continent at least, and as far as I can detect, today exercises no power whatever over the rank and file of Bible-believing Christians. For this there may be a number of contributing factors; but the chief one is, I believe, the misfortune suffered by prophetic truth between the two world wars when men without tears undertook to instruct us in the writings of the tear-stained prophets. Big crowds and big offerings resulted until event proved the teachers wrong on too many points; then the reaction set in and prophecy lost favor with the masses. This was a neat trick of the devil and it worked too well. We should and must learn that we cannot handle holy things carelessly without suffering serious consequences.

Another field where tearless men have done us untold harm is in prayer for the sick. There have always been reverent, serious men who felt it their sacred duty to pray for the sick that they might be healed in the will of God. It was said of Spurgeon that his prayers raised up more sick persons than the ministrations of any doctor in London. When tearless promoters took up the doctrine it was turned into a lucrative racket. Smooth, persuasive men used superior salesmanship methods to make impressive fortunes out of their campaigns. Their big ranches and heavy financial investments prove how successful they have been in separating the sick and suffering from their money. And this in the name of the Man of Sorrows who had not where to lay His head!

Whatever is done without heart is done in the dark no matter how scriptural it may appear to be. By the law of just compensation the heart of the religious trifler will be destroyed by the exceeding brightness of the truth he touches. Tearless eyes are finally blinded by the light at which they gaze.

We of the nonliturgical churches tend to look with some disdain upon those churches that follow a carefully prescribed form of service, and certainly there must be a good deal in such services that has little or no meaning for the average participant—this not because it is carefully prescribed but because the average participant is what he is. But I have observed that our familiar impromptu service, planned by the leader twenty minutes before, often tends to follow a ragged and tired order almost as standardized as the Mass. The liturgical service is at least beautiful; ours is often ugly. Theirs has been carefully worked out through the centuries to capture as much of beauty as possible and to preserve a spirit of reverence among the worshipers. Ours is often an off-the-cuff makeshift with nothing to recommend it. Its so-called liberty is often not liberty at all but sheer slovenliness.

The theory is that if the meeting is unplanned the Holy Spirit will work freely, and that would be true if all the worshipers were reverent and Spirit-filled. But mostly there is neither order nor Spirit, just a routine prayer that is, except for minor variations, the same week after week, and a few songs that were never much to start with and have long ago lost all significance by meaningless repetition.

In the majority of our meetings there is scarcely a trace of reverent thought, no recognition of the unity of the body, little sense of the divine Presence, no moment of stillness, no solemnity, no wonder, no holy fear. But so often there is a dull or a breezy song leader full of awkward jokes, as well as a chairman announcing each "number" with the old radio continuity patter in an effort to make everything hang together.

The whole Christian family stands desperately in need of a restoration of penitence, humility and tears. May God send them soon.

12

The Vital Place of the Church

The highest expression of the will of God in this age is the church which He purchased with His own blood. To be scripturally valid any religious activity must be part of the church. Let it be clearly stated that there can be no service acceptable to God in this age that does not center in and spring out of the church. Bible schools, tract societies, Christian business men's committees, seminaries, and the many independent groups working at one or another phase of religion need to check themselves reverently and courageously, for they have no true spiritual significance outside of or apart from the church.

According to the Scriptures the church is the habitation of God through the Spirit, and as such is the most important organism beneath the sun. She is not one more good institution along with the home, the state, and the school; she is the most vital of all institutions—the only one that can claim a heavenly origin.

The cynic may inquire which church we mean, and may remind us that the Christian church is so divided that it is impossible to tell which is the true one, even if such a one exists. But we are not too much troubled by the suppressed smile of the doubter. Being inside the church we are probably as well aware of her faults as any person on the outside could possibly be. And we believe in her nevertheless wherever she manifests herself in a world of darkness and unbelief.

The church is found wherever the Holy Spirit has drawn together a few persons who trust Christ for their salvation, worship God in spirit and have no dealings with the world and the flesh. The members may by necessity be scattered over the surface of the earth and separated by distance and circumstances, but in every true member of the church is the homing instinct and the longing of the sheep for the fold and the shepherd. Give a few real Christians half a chance and they will get together and organize and plan regular meetings for prayer and worship. In these meetings they will hear the Scriptures expounded, break bread together in one form or another according to their light, and try as far as possible to spread the saving gospel to the lost world.

Such groups are cells in the Body of Christ, and each one is a true church, a real part of the greater church. It is in and through these cells that the Spirit does His work on earth. Whoever scorns the local church scorns the Body of Christ.

The church is still to be reckoned with. "The gates of hell shall not prevail against her."

13

Organization: Necessary and Dangerous

Basically, organization is the placing of several parts of a whole in such relation to each other that a desired end may be achieved. This may be by consent or compulsion, depending upon the circumstances.

A certain amount of organization is necessary everywhere throughout the created universe and in all human society. Without it there could be no science, no government, no family unit, no art, no music, no literature, no creative activity of any kind.

Life requires organization. There is no such thing as life apart from the medium through which it expresses itself. It cannot exist as a thing in itself independent of an organized body. It is found only where there is some body, some form in which it may reside. And where there is body and form there is organization. A man, for instance, is the sum of his organized and coordinated parts and in these and through these the mystery of life is afforded expression. When, for any cause, the parts become disorganized life departs and the man dies.

Society requires organization. If men are to live together in the world they must be organized in some manner. This has been recognized in all times and places and is seen on all levels of human society from the jungle tribe to the world empire. Ideally the object of government is to achieve order with a minimum of restraint while permitting a maximum of freedom to the individual.

That some restraint of individual liberty is good and necessary is admitted by all intelligent persons; that too much restraint is bad is also admitted by everyone. Disagreement arises when we try to define "some" and "too much." Just how much is too much? and how little is some? If this could be settled peace would descend upon Congress and Parliament, the Democrat and the liberal would lie down with the Republican and the conservative, and a little child should lead them.

The difference between the slave state and the free is one of degree only. Even the totalitarian countries enjoy some freedom, and the citizens of the free nations must endure a certain amount of restraint. It is the balance between the two that decides whether a given country is slave or free. No informed citizen believes he is absolutely free. He knows his liberty must be curtailed somewhat for the benefit of all. The best he can hope for is that the curtailment will be kept at a minimum. This minimum of curtailment he calls "freedom," and so precious is it that he is willing to risk his life for it. The Western world fought two major wars within twenty-five years to preserve this balance of liberty and escape the tighter restrictions that Nazism and Facism would have imposed upon it.

Being Christ-centered and church-oriented in his thinking, this writer of course relates everything to the Christian religion. I am and have been for years much distressed about the tendency to over-organize the Christian community, and I have for that reason had it charged against me that I do not believe in organization. The truth is quite otherwise.

The man who would oppose all organization in the church must needs be ignorant of the facts of life. Art is organized beauty; music is organized sound; philosophy is organized thought; science is organized knowledge; government is merely society organized. And what is the true church of Christ but organized mystery?

The throbbing heart of the church is life—in the happy

phrase of Henry Scougal, "the life of God in the soul of man." This life, together with the actual presence of Christ within her, constitutes the church a divine thing, a mystery, a miracle. Yet without substance, form and order this divine life would have no dwelling place, and no way to express itself to the community.

For this reason there is much in the New Testament about organization. Paul's pastoral epistles and his letters to the Corinthian Christians reveal that the great apostle was an organizer. He reminded Titus that he had left him in Crete to set in order the things that were wanting and to ordain elders in every city. Surely this can only mean that Titus was commissioned by the apostle to impose some kind of order upon the various companies of believers living in the island, and order can only be achieved through organization.

Christians have tended to err in one of several directions because they have not understood the purpose of organization or the dangers that attend it if it is allowed to get out of hand. Some will have no organization at all, and of course the results are confusion and disorder, and these can never help mankind or bring glory to our Lord. Others substitute organization for life, and while having a name to live they are dead. Still others become so enamored of rules and regulations that they multiply them beyond all reason, and soon the spontaneity is smothered within the church and the life squeezed out of it.

It is with the latter error that I am mainly concerned. Many church groups have perished from too much organization, even as others from too little. Wise church leaders will watch out for both extremes. A man may die as a result of having too low blood pressure as certainly as from having too high, and it matters little which takes him off. He is equally dead either way. The important thing in church organization is to discover the scriptural balance between two extremes and avoid both.

It is painful to see a happy group of Christians, born in

simplicity and held together by the bonds of heavenly love, slowly lose their simple character, begin to try to regulate every sweet impulse of the Spirit and slowly die from within. Yet that is the direction almost all Christian denominations have taken throughout history, and in spite of the warnings set out by the Holy Spirit and the Scriptures of truth it is the direction almost all church groups are taking today.

While there is some danger that our present-day evangelical groups may suffer from want of proper organization, the real peril surely lies on the other side. Churches run toward complexity as ducks take to water. What is back of this?

First, I think it arises from a natural but carnal desire on the part of a gifted minority to bring the less gifted majority to heel and get them where they will not stand in the way of their soaring ambitions. The oftquoted (and usually misquoted) saying is true in religion as well as in politics: "Power tends to corrupt and absolute power tends to corrupt absolutely." The itch to have the preeminence is one disease for which no natural cure has ever been found.

Another cause back of our top-heavy and ugly overorganization is fear. Churches and societies founded by saintly men with courage, faith and sanctified imagination appear unable to propagate themselves on the same spiritual level beyond one or two generations. The spiritual fathers were not able to sire others with courage and faith equal to their own. The fathers had God and little else, but their descendants lose their vision and look to methods and constitutions for the power their hearts tell them they lack. Then rules and precedents harden into a protective shell where they can take refuge from trouble. It is always easier and safer to pull in our necks than to fight things out on the field of battle.

In all our fallen life there is a strong gravitational pull toward complexity and away from things simple and real.

There seems to be a kind of sad inevitability back of our morbid urge toward spiritual suicide. Only by prophetic insight, watchful prayer and hard work can we reverse the trend and recover the departed glory.

In the old cemetery near historic Plymouth Rock where sleep the Pilgrim Fathers, there is a stone into which has been carved these solemn words (I quote from memory): "That which our fathers at such a great price secured, let us not lightly cast away."

We mid-century evangelicals might be wise to apply these words to our own religious situation. We are still Protestants. We must protest the light casting away of our religious freedom. The simple liberty of early Christianity is being lost to us. One by one we are surrendering those rights purchased for us by the blood of the everlasting covenant—the right to be ourselves, the right to obey the Holy Spirit, the right to think our own private thoughts, the right to do what we will with our lives, the right to determine under God what we shall do with our money.

And remember, our dangers for the moment come not from without, but from within.

14

Divisions Are Not Always Bad

When to unite and when to divide, that is the question, and a right answer requires the wisdom of a Solomon.

Some settle the problem by rule of thumb: All union is good and all division bad. It's that easy. But obviously this effortless way of dealing with the matter ignores the lessons of history and overlooks some of the deep spiritual laws by which men live.

If good men were all for union and bad men for division, or vice versa, that would simplify things for us. Or if it could be shown that God always unites and the devil always divides it would be easy to find our way around in this confused and confusing world. But that is not how things are.

To divide what should be divided and unite what should be united is the part of wisdom. Union of dissimilar elements is never good even where it is possible, nor is the arbitrary division of elements that are alike; and this is as certainly true of things moral and religious as of things political or scientific.

The first divider was God who at the creation divided the light from the darkness. This division set the direction for all God's dealings in nature and in grace. Light and darkness are incompatible; to try to have both in the same place at once is to try the impossible and end by having neither the one nor the other, but dimness rather, and obscurity.

In the world of men there are at present scarcely any sharp outlines. The race is fallen. Sin has brought confusion. The wheat grows with the tares, the sheep and the goats coexist, the farms of the just and the unjust lie side by side in the landscape, the mission is next door to the saloon.

But things will not always be so. The hour is coming when the sheep will be divided from the goats and the tares separated from the wheat. God will again divide the light from the darkness and all things will run to their kind. Tares will go into the fire with tares and wheat into the garner with wheat. The dimness will lift like a fog and all outlines will appear. Hell will be seen to be hell all the way through, and heaven revealed as the one home of all who bear the nature of the one God.

For that time we with patience wait. In the meanwhile for each of us, and for the church wherever she appears in human society, the constantly recurring question must be: What shall we unite with and from what shall we separate? The question of coexistence does not enter here, but the question of union and fellowship does. The wheat grows in the same field with the tares, but shall the two cross-pollinate? The sheep graze near the goats, but shall they seek to interbreed? The unjust and the just enjoy the same rain and sunshine, but shall they forget their deep moral differences and intermarry?

To these questions the popular answer is *yes*. Union for union's sake, and men shall brothers be for a' that. Unity is so devoutly to be desired that no price is too high to pay for it and nothing is important enough to keep us apart. Truth is slain to provide a feast to celebrate the marriage of heaven and hell, and all to support a concept of unity which has no basis in the Word of God.

The Spirit-illuminated church will have none of this. In a fallen world like ours unity is no treasure to be purchased at the price of compromise. Loyalty to God, faithfulness to truth and the preservation of a good conscience are jewels more precious than gold of Ophir or diamonds from the mine. For these jewels men have suffered the loss of property, imprisonment and even death; for them, even in recent times, behind the various curtains, followers of Christ have paid the last full measure of devotion and quietly died, unknown to and unsung by the great world, but known to God and dear to His Father heart. In the day that shall declare the secrets of all souls these shall come forth to receive the deeds done in the body. Surely such as these are wiser philosophers than the religious camp followers of meaningless unity who have not the courage to stand against current vogues and who bleat for brotherhood only because it happens to be for the time popular.

"Divide and conquer" is the cynical slogan of Machiavellian political leaders, but Satan knows also how to *unite* and conquer. To bring a nation to its knees the aspiring dictator must unite it. By repeated appeals to national pride or to the need to avenge some past or present wrong the demagogue succeeds in uniting the populace behind him. It is easy after that to take control of the military and to beat the legislature into submission. Then follows almost perfect unity indeed, but it is the unity of the stockyards and the concentration camp. We have seen this happen several times in this century, and the world will see it at least once more when the nations of the earth are united under Antichrist.

When confused sheep start over a cliff the individual sheep can save himself only by separating from the flock. Perfect unity at such a time can only mean total destruction for all. The wise sheep to save his own hide disaffiliates.

Power lies in the union of things similar and the division of things dissimilar. Maybe what we need in religious circles today is not more union but some wise and courageous division. Everyone desires peace but it could be that revival will follow the sword.

15

The Responsibility of Leadership

The history of Israel and Judah points up a truth taught clearly enough by *all* history, viz., that the masses are or soon will be what their leaders are. The kings set the moral pace for the people.

The public is never capable of acting en masse. Without a leader it is headless and a headless body is powerless. Always someone must lead. Even the mob engaged in pillage and murder is not the disorganized thing it appears to be. Somewhere behind the violence is a leader whose ideas it is simply putting into effect.

Israel sometimes rebelled against her leaders, it is true, but the rebellions were not spontaneous. The people merely switched to a new leader and followed him. The point is, they always had to have a leader.

Whatever sort of man the king turned out to be, the people were soon following his leadership. They followed David in the worship of Jehovah, Solomon in the building of the Temple, Jeroboam in the making of a calf and Hezekiah in the restoration of the temple worship.

It is not complimentary to the masses that they are so easily led, but we are not interested in praising or blaming; we are concerned for truth, and the truth is that for better or for worse religious people follow leaders. A good man may change the moral complexion of a whole nation; or a corrupt and worldly clergy may lead a nation into bondage. The transposed proverb, "Like priest, like people," sums up in four words a truth taught plainly in the Scriptures and demonstrated again and again in religious history.

Today Christianity in the Western world is what its leaders were in the recent past and is becoming what its present leaders are. The local church soon becomes like its pastor, and this is true even of those groups who do not believe in pastors. The true pastor of such a group is not hard to identify; he is usually the one who can present the strongest argument against any church having a pastor. The strong-minded leader of the local group who succeeds in influencing the flock through Bible teaching or frequent impromptu talks in the public gatherings is the pastor, no matter how earnestly he may deny it.

The poor condition of the churches today may be traced straight to their leaders. When, as sometimes happens, the members of a local church rise up and turn their pastor out for preaching the truth, they are still following a leader. Behind their act is sure to be found a carnal (and often well-to-do) deacon or elder who usurps the right to determine who the pastor shall be and what he shall say twice each Sunday. In such cases the pastor is unable to lead the flock. He merely *works* for the leader; a pitiful situation indeed.

A number of factors contribute to bad spiritual leadership. Here are a few:

1. *Fear.* The wish to be liked and admired is strong even among the clergy, so rather than risk public disapproval the pastor is tempted simply to sit on his hands and smile ingratiatingly at the people. "The fear of man bringeth a snare," says the Holy Spirit, and nowhere more than in the ministry.

2. *The economic squeeze.* The Protestant ministry is notoriously underpaid and the pastor's family is often large. Put these two facts together and you have a situation ready-made to bring trouble and temptation to the man of God. The ability of the congregation to turn off the flow

of money to the church when the man in the pulpit gets on their toes is well known. The average pastor lives from year to year, barely making ends meet. To give vigorous moral leadership to the church is often to invite economic strangulation, so such leadership is withheld. But the evil thing is that *leadership withheld is in fact a kind of inverted leadership*. The man who will not lead his flock up the mountainside leads it down without knowing it.

3. *Ambition*. When Christ is not all in all to the minister he is tempted to seek place for himself, and pleasing the crowds is a time-proved way to get on in church circles. Instead of leading his people where they ought to go he skillfully leads them where he knows they *want* to go. In this way he gives the appearance of being a bold leader of men, but avoids offending anyone, and thus assures ecclesiastical preferment when the big church or the high office is open.

4. *Intellectual pride*. Unfortunately there is in religious circles a cult of the intelligentsia which, in my opinion, is merely beatnikism turned wrong side out. As the beatnik, in spite of his loud protestations of individualism, is in reality one of the most slavish of conformists, so the young intellectual in the pulpit shakes in his carefully polished Oxfords lest he be guilty of saying something trite or common. The people look to him to lead them into green pastures but instead he leads them to a sandy desert.

5. *Absence of true spiritual experience*. No one can lead another farther than he himself has gone. For many ministers this explains their failure to lead. They simply do not know where to go.

6. *Inadequate preparation*. The churches are cluttered with religious amateurs culturally unfit to minister at the altar, and the people suffer as a consequence. They are led astray and are not aware of it.

The rewards of godly leadership are so great and the responsibilities of the leader so heavy that no one can afford to take the matter lightly.

16

The Prayer of a Minor Prophet

This is the prayer of a man called to be a witness to the nations. This is what he said to his Lord on the day of his ordination. After the elders and ministers had prayed and laid their hands on him he withdrew to meet his Saviour in the secret place and in the silence, farther in than his well-meaning brethren could take him.

And he said: O Lord, I have heard Thy voice and was afraid. Thou hast called me to an awesome task in a grave and perilous hour. Thou art about to shake all nations and the earth and also heaven, that the things that cannot be shaken may remain. O Lord, my Lord, Thou hast stooped to honor me to be Thy servant. No man taketh this honor upon himself save he that is called of God as was Aaron. Thou hast ordained me Thy messenger to them that are stubborn of heart and hard of hearing. They have rejected Thee, the Master, and it is not to be expected that they will receive me, the servant.

My God, I shall not waste time deploring my weakness nor my unfittedness for the work. The responsibility is not mine, but Thine. Thou hast said, "I knew thee—I ordained thee—I sanctified thee," and Thou hast also said, "Thou shalt go to all that I shall send thee, and whatsoever I command thee thou shalt speak." Who am I to argue with Thee or to call into question Thy sovereign choice? The decision is not mine but Thine. So be it, Lord. Thy will, not mine, be done.

Well do I know, Thou God of the prophets and the apostles, that as long as I honor Thee Thou wilt honor me. Help me therefore to take this solemn vow to honor Thee in all my future life and labors, whether by gain or by loss, by life or by death, and then to keep that vow unbroken while I live.

It is time, O God, for Thee to work, for the enemy has entered into Thy pastures and the sheep are torn and scattered. And false shepherds abound who deny the danger and laugh at the perils which surround Thy flock. The sheep are deceived by these hirelings and follow them with touching loyalty while the wolf closes in to kill and destroy. I beseech Thee, give me sharp eyes to detect the presence of the enemy; give me understanding to see and courage to report what I see faithfully. Make my voice so like Thine own that even the sick sheep will recognize it and follow Thee.

Lord Jesus, I come to Thee for spiritual preparation. Lay Thy hand upon me. Anoint me with the oil of the New Testament prophet. Forbid that I should become a religious scribe and thus lose my prophetic calling. Save me from the curse that lies dark across the face of the modern clergy, the curse of compromise, of imitation, of professionalism. Save me from the error of judging a church by its size, its popularity or the amount of its yearly offering. Help me to remember that I am a prophet—not a promoter, not a religious manager, but a prophet. Let me never become a slave to crowds. Heal my soul of carnal ambitions and deliver me from the itch for publicity. Save me from bondage to things. Let me not waste my days puttering around the house. Lay Thy terror upon me, O God, and drive me to the place of prayer where I may wrestle with principalities and powers and the rulers of the darkness of this world. Deliver me from overeating and late sleeping. Teach me self-discipline that I may be a good soldier of Jesus Christ.

I accept hard work and small rewards in this life. I ask

for no easy place. I shall try to be blind to the little ways that could make life easier. If others seek the smoother path I shall try to take the hard way without judging them too harshly. I shall expect opposition and try to take it quietly when it comes. Or if, as sometimes it falleth out to Thy servants, I should have grateful gifts pressed upon me by Thy kindly people, stand by me then and save me from the blight that often follows. Teach me to use whatever I receive in such manner that will not injure my soul nor diminish my spiritual power. And if in Thy permissive providence honor should come to me from Thy church, let me not forget in that hour that I am unworthy of the least of Thy mercies, and that if men knew me as intimately as I know myself they would withhold their honors or bestow them upon others more worthy to receive them.

And now, O Lord of heaven and earth, I consecrate my remaining days to Thee; let them be many or few, as Thou wilt. Let me stand before the great or minister to the poor and lowly; that choice is not mine, and I would not influence it if I could. I am Thy servant to do Thy will, and that will is sweeter to me than position or riches or fame and I choose it above all things on earth or in heaven.

Though I am chosen of Thee and honored by a high and holy calling, let me never forget that I am but a man of dust and ashes, a man with all the natural faults and passions that plague the race of men. I pray Thee, therefore, my Lord and Redeemer, save me from myself and from all the injuries I may do myself while trying to be a blessing to others. Fill me with Thy power by the Holy Spirit, and I will go in Thy strength and tell of Thy righteousness, even Thine only. I will spread abroad the message of redeeming love while my normal powers endure.

Then, dear Lord, when I am old and weary and too tired to go on, have a place ready for me above, and make me to be numbered with Thy saints in glory everlasting. *Amen.* AMEN.

17

Wanted: Courage with Moderation

Sin has done a pretty complete job of ruining us and the process of restoration is long and slow.

The works of grace in the individual life may be never so clear and definite, but it is indeed the labor of a God to bring the once fallen heart back into the divine likeness again. In nothing is this seen more plainly than in the great difficulty we experience in achieving spiritual symmetry in our lives. The inability of even the most devout souls to show forth the Christian virtues in equal proportion and without admixture of unChristlike qualities has been the source of heartache to many of God's believing people.

The virtues before us, courage and moderation, when held in correct proportion, make for a well-balanced life and one of great usefulness in the kingdom of God. Where one is missing or present only in minute degree, the result is a life out of balance and powers wasted.

Almost any sincere writing, if examined closely, will be found to be autobiographic. We know best what we have ourselves experienced. This article is not an exception. I may as well admit frankly that it is autobiographic, for the discerning reader will discover the truth no matter how hard I may try to conceal it.

Briefly, I have seldom been called a coward, even by my most cordial enemies, but my want of moderation has sometimes caused grief to my dearest friends. An extreme

This chapter appeared in *The Alliance Witness* (then *Weekly*) in July, 1946.

disposition is not easy to tame, and the temptation to bring severe, immoderate methods to the aid of the Lord is one not easily resisted. The temptation is further strengthened by the knowledge that it is next to impossible to pin a preacher down and make him eat his words. There is a ministerial immunity accorded a man of God which may lead Boanerges into extravagant and irresponsible language unless he uses heroic measures to bring his nature under the sway of the Spirit of love. This I have sometimes failed to do, and always to my own real sorrow.

Here again the contrast between the ways of God and the ways of man is seen. Apart from such wisdom as painful experience may give, we are prone to try to secure our ends by direct attack, to rush the field and win by assault. That was Samson's way, and it worked well except for one minor oversight: it slew the victor along with the vanquished! There is a wisdom in the flank attack, but a wisdom which the rash spirit is likely to reject.

Of Christ it was said, "He shall not strive, nor cry; neither shall any man hear his voice in the streets. A bruised reed shall he not break, and smoking flax shall he not quench, till he send forth judgment into victory." He achieved His tremendous purposes without undue physical exertion and altogether without violence. His whole life was marked by moderation; yet He was of all men the most utterly courageous. He could send back word to Herod who had threatened Him, "Go ye, and tell that fox, Behold, I cast out devils, and I do cures today and tomorrow, and the third day I shall be perfected." There is consummate courage here, but no defiance, no sign of contempt, no extravagance of word or act. He had courage with moderation.

The failure to achieve balance between these virtues has caused much evil in the church through the years, and the injury is all the greater when church leaders are involved. Lack of courage is a grave fault and may be a real sin when it leads to compromise in doctrine or practice. To sit back for the sake of peace and allow the enemy to carry off the sacred vessels from the temple is never the part of a true man of God. Moderation to the point of surrender where holy things are concerned is certainly not a virtue; but pugnacity never yet won when the battle was a heavenly one. The fury of man never furthered the glory of God. There is a right way to do things, and it is never the violent way. The Greeks had a famous saying: "Moderation is best"; and the homely proverb of the American farmer, "Easy does it," has in it a wealth of profound philosophy.

God has used, and undoubtedly will yet use men in spite of their failure to hold these qualities in proper balance. Elijah was a man of courage; no one could doubt that, but neither would anyone be so rash as to claim that he was a man of patience or moderation. He carried the day by assault, by challenge, and was not above satire and abuse when he thought it would help things; but when the enemy was confounded he went into a tailspin and sank into the depths of despair. That is the way of the extreme nature, of the man of courage without moderation.

Eli, on the other hand, was a man of moderation. He could not say "no" even to his own family. He loved a weak peace, and stark tragedy was the price he paid for his cowardice. Both these men were good men, but they could not find the happy mean. Of the two, the fiery Elijah was certainly the greater man. It is painful to think what Eli would have done in Elijah's circumstances. And I could pity even Hophni and Phinehas if Elijah had been their father!

This leads us logically to think of Paul, the apostle. Here is a man whom we need never take at a discount. He seems to have had an almost perfect courage along with a patient disposition and a forbearance truly Godlike. What he might have been apart from grace is seen in the brief description given of him before his conversion. After he had helped to stone Stephen to death, he went out Christian hunting, "breathing out threatenings and slaughter." Even after his conversion he was capable of summary judgments when he felt strongly on a question. His curt rejection of Mark after he had gone back from the work was an example of his short way of dealing with men in whom he had lost confidence. But time and suffering and an increasing intimacy with the patient Saviour seems to have cured this fault in the man of God. His later days were sweet with love and fragrant with forbearance and charity. So should it be with all of us.

It is a significant thing that the Bible gives no record of a coward ever being cured of his malady. No "timid soul" ever grew into a man of courage. Peter is sometimes cited as an exception, but there is nothing in his record that would mark him as a timid man either before or after Pentecost. He did touch the borderline once or twice, it is true, but for the most part he was a man of such explosive courage that he was forever in trouble by his boldness.

How desperately the church at this moment needs men of courage is too well known to need repetition. Fear broods over the church like some ancient curse. Fear for our living, fear of our jobs, fear of losing popularity, fear of each other: these are the ghosts that haunt the men who stand today in places of church leadership. Many of them, however, win a reputation for courage by repeating safe and expected things with comical daring.

Yet self-conscious courage is not the cure. To cultivate the habit of "calling a spade a spade" may merely result in our making a nuisance of ourselves and doing a lot of damage in the process. The ideal seems to be a quiet courage that is not aware of its own presence. It draws its strength each moment from the indwelling Spirit and is hardly aware of *self* at all. Such a courage will be patient also and well-balanced and safe from extremes. May God send a baptism of such courage upon us.

18

This World: Playground or Battleground?

Things are for us not only what they are; they are what we hold them to be. Which is to say that our attitude toward things is likely in the long run to be more important than the things themselves.

This is a common coin of knowledge, like an old dime, worn smooth by use. Yet it bears upon it the stamp of truth and must not be rejected because it is familiar.

It is strange how a fact may remain fixed, while our interpretation of the fact changes with the generations and the years.

One such fact is the world in which we live. It is here, and has been here through the centuries. It is a stable fact, quite unchanged by the passing of time, but how different is modern man's view of it from the view our fathers held. Here we see plainly how great is the power of interpretation. The world is for all of us not only what it is; it is what we believe it to be. And a tremendous load of woe or weal rides on the soundness of our interpretation.

Going no further back than the times of the founding and early development of our country we are able to see the wide gulf between our modern attitudes and those of our fathers. In the early days, when Christianity exercised a dominant influence over American thinking, men conceived the world to be a battleground. Our fathers believed in sin and the devil and hell as constituting one force; and they believed in God and righteousness and heaven as the other. These were opposed to each other in the nature of them forever in deep, grave, irreconcilable hostility. Man, so our fathers held, had to choose sides; he could not be neutral. For him it must be life or death, heaven or hell, and if he chose to come out on God's side he could expect open war with God's enemies. The fight would be real and deadly and would last as long as life continued here below. Men looked forward to heaven as a return from the wars, a laying down of the sword to enjoy in peace the home prepared for them.

Sermons and songs in those days often had a martial quality about them, or perhaps a trace of homesickness. The Christian soldier thought of home and rest and re-union, and his voice grew plaintive as he sang of battle ended and victory won. But whether he was charging into enemy guns or dreaming of war's end and the Father's welcome home, he never forgot what kind of world he lived in. It was a battleground, and many were the wound-ed and the slain.

That view of things is unquestionably the scriptural one. Allowing for the figures and metaphors with which the Scriptures abound, it still is a solid Bible doctrine that tremendous spiritual forces are present in the world, and man, because of his spiritual nature, is caught in the middle. The evil powers are bent upon destroying him, while Christ is present to save him through the power of the gospel. To obtain deliverance he must come out on God's side in faith and obedience. That in brief is what our fathers thought; and that, we believe, is what the Bible teaches.

How different today: the fact remains the same but the interpretation has changed completely. Men think of the world, not as a battleground but as a playground. We are not here to fight, we are here to frolic. We are not in a foreign land, we are at home. We are not getting ready to live, we are already living, and the best we can do is to rid ourselves of our inhibitions and our frustrations and live this life to the full. This, we believe, is a fair summary of the religious philosophy of modern man, openly professed by millions and tacitly held by more multiplied millions who live out that philosophy without having given verbal expression to it.

This changed attitude toward the world has had and is having its effect upon Christians, even gospel Christians who profess the faith of the Bible. By a curious juggling of the figures they manage to add up the column wrong and yet claim to have the right answer. It sounds fantastic but it is true.

That this world is a playground instead of a battle-ground has now been accepted in practice by the vast majority of evangelical Christians. They might hedge around the question if they were asked bluntly to declare their position, but their conduct gives them away. They are facing both ways, enjoying Christ and the world too, and gleefully telling everyone that accepting Jesus does not require them to give up their fun, and that Christianity is just the jolliest thing imaginable.

The "worship" growing out of such a view of life is as far off center as the view itself, a sort of sanctified night clubbing without the champagne and the dressed-up drunks.

This whole thing has grown to be so serious of late that it now becomes the bounden duty of every Christian to reexamine his spiritual philosophy in the light of the Bible, and having discovered the scriptural way to follow it, even if to do so he must separate himself from much that he formerly accepted as real but which now in the light of truth he knows to be false.

A right view of God and the world to come requires that we have also a right view of the world in which we live and our relation to it. So much depends upon this that we cannot afford to be careless about it.

19
The Waning Authority of Christ in the Churches

Here is the burden of my heart; and while I claim for myself no special inspiration I yet feel that this is also the burden of the Spirit.

If I know my own heart it is love alone that moves me to write this. What I write here is not the sour ferment of a mind agitated by contentions with my fellow Christians. There have been no such contentions. I have not been abused, mistreated or attacked by anyone. Nor have these observations grown out of any unpleasant experiences that I have had in my association with others. My relations with my own church as well as with Christians of other denominations have been friendly, courteous and pleasant. My grief is simply the result of a condition which I believe to be almost universally prevalent among the churches.

I think also that I should acknowledge that I am myself very much involved in the situation I here deplore. As Ezra in his mighty prayer of intercession included himself among the wrongdoers, so do I. "O my God, I am ashamed and blush to lift up my face to thee, my God: for our iniquities are increased over our head, and our trespass is grown up unto the heavens." Any hard word spoken here against others must in simple honesty return upon my own head. I too have been guilty. This is written with the hope that we all may turn unto the Lord our God and sin no more against Him.

This article first appeared in *The Alliance Witness* on May 15, 1963, just two days after the death of Dr. Tozer. In a sense it was his valedictory, for it expressed the concern of his heart.

Let me state the cause of my burden. It is this: *Jesus Christ has today almost no authority at all among the groups that call themselves by His name.* By these I mean not the Roman Catholics nor the liberals, nor the various quasi-Christian cults. I do mean Protestant churches generally, and I include those that protest the loudest that they are in spiritual descent from our Lord and His apostles, namely, the evangelicals.

It is a basic doctrine of the New Testament that after His resurrection the Man Jesus was declared by God to be both Lord and Christ, and that He was invested by the Father with absolute Lordship over the church which is His Body. All authority is His in heaven and in earth. In His own proper time He will exert it to the full, but during this period in history He allows this authority to be challenged or ignored. And just now it is being challenged by the world and ignored by the church.

The present position of Christ in the gospel churches may be likened to that of a king in a limited, constitutional monarchy. The king (sometimes depersonalized by the term "the Crown") is in such a country no more than a traditional rallying point, a pleasant symbol of unity and loyalty much like a flag or a national anthem. He is lauded, feted and supported, but his real authority is small. Nominally he is head over all, but in every crisis someone else makes the decisions. On formal occasions he appears in his royal attire to deliver the tame, colorless speech put into his mouth by the real rulers of the country. The whole thing may be no more than good-natured make-believe, but it is rooted in antiquity—it is a lot of fun and no one wants to give it up.

Among the gospel churches Christ is now in fact little more than a beloved symbol. "All Hail the Power of Jesus' Name" is the church's national anthem and the cross is her official flag, but in the week-by-week services of the church and the day-by-day conduct of her members someone else, not Christ, makes the decisions. Under proper circumstances Christ is allowed to say "Come unto me, all ye that labour and are heavy laden" or "Let not your heart be troubled," but when the speech is finished someone else takes over. Those in actual authority decide the moral standards of the church, as well as all objectives and all methods employed to achieve them. Because of long and meticulous organization it is now possible for the youngest pastor just out of seminary to have more actual authority in a church than Jesus Christ has.

Not only does Christ have little or no authority; His influence also is becoming less and less. I would not say that He has none, only that it is small and diminishing. A fair parallel would be the influence of Abraham Lincoln over the American people. Honest Abe is still the idol of the country. The likeness of his kind, rugged face, so homely that it is beautiful, appears everywhere. It is easy to grow misty-eyed over him. Children are brought up on stories of his love, his honesty and his humility.

But after we have gotten control over our tender emotions what have we left? No more than a good example which, as it recedes into the past, becomes more and more unreal and exercises less and less real influence. Every scoundrel is ready to wrap Lincoln's long, black coat around him. In the cold light of political facts in the United States the constant appeal to Lincoln by the politicians is a cynical joke.

The Lordship of Jesus is not quite forgotten among Christians, but it has been relegated to the hymnal where all responsibility toward it may be comfortably discharged in a glow of pleasant religious emotion. Or if it is taught as a theory in the classroom it is rarely applied to practical living. The idea that the Man Christ Jesus has absolute and final authority over the whole church and over all of its members in every detail of their lives is simply not now accepted as true by the rank and file of evangelical Christians.

What we do is this: We accept the Christianity of our

group as being identical with that of Christ and His apostles. The beliefs, the practices, the ethics, the activities of our group are equated with the Christianity of the New Testament. Whatever the group thinks or says or does is scriptural, no questions asked. It is assumed that all our Lord expects of us is that we busy ourselves with the activities of the group. In so doing we are keeping the commandments of Christ.

To avoid the hard necessity of either obeying or rejecting the plain instructions of our Lord in the New Testament we take refuge in a liberal interpretation of them. Casuistry is not the possession of Roman Catholic theologians alone. We evangelicals also know how to avoid the sharp point of obedience by means of fine and intricate explanations. These are tailor-made for the flesh. They excuse disobedience, comfort carnality and make the words of Christ of none effect. And the essence of it all is that Christ simply could not have meant what He said. His teachings are accepted even theoretically only after they have been weakened by interpretation.

Yet Christ is consulted by increasing numbers of persons with "problems" and sought after by those who long for peace of mind. He is widely recommended as a kind of spiritual psychiatrist with remarkable powers to straighten people out. He is able to deliver them from their guilt complexes and to help them to avoid serious psychic traumas by making a smooth and easy adjustment to society and to their own ids. Of course this strange Christ has no relation whatever to the Christ of the New Testament. The true Christ is also Lord, but this accommodating Christ is little more than the servant of the people.

But I suppose I should offer some concrete proof to support my charge that Christ has little or no authority today among the churches. Well, let me put a few questions and let the answers be the evidence.

What church board consults our Lord's words to decide matters under discussion? Let anyone reading this who

has had experience on a church board try to recall the
times or time when any board member read from the
Scriptures to make a point, or when any chairman sug-
gested that the brethren should see what instructions the
Lord had for them on a particular question. Board meetings are habitually opened with a formal prayer or "a season of prayer"; after that the Head of the Church is
respectfully silent while the real rulers take over. Let anyone who denies this bring forth evidence to refute it. I for
one will be glad to hear it.

What Sunday school committee goes to the Word for
directions? Do not the members invariably assume that
they already know what they are supposed to do and that
their only problem is to find effective means to get it
done? Plans, rules, "operations" and new methodological
techniques absorb all their time and attention. The prayer
before the meeting is for divine help to carry out their
plans. Apparently the idea that the Lord might have some
instructions for them never so much as enters their heads.

Who remembers when a conference chairman brought
his Bible to the table with him for the purpose of using it?
Minutes, regulations, rules of order, yes. The sacred commandments of the Lord, no. An absolute dichotomy exists
between the devotional period and the business session.
The first has no relation to the second.

What foreign mission board actually seeks to follow the
guidance of the Lord as provided by His Word and His
Spirit? They all think they do, but what they do in fact is
to assume the scripturalness of their ends and then ask for
help to find ways to achieve them. They may pray all
night for God to give success to their enterprises, but
Christ is desired as their helper, not as their Lord. Human
means are devised to achieve ends assumed to be divine.
These harden into policy, and thereafter the Lord doesn't
even have a vote.

In the conduct of our public worship where is the authority of Christ to be found? The truth is that today the

Lord rarely controls a service, and the influence He exerts is very small. We sing of Him and preach about Him, but He must not interfere; we worship our way, and it must be right because we have always done it that way, as have the other churches in our group.

What Christian when faced with a moral problem goes straight to the Sermon on the Mount or other New Testament Scripture for the authoritative answer? Who lets the words of Christ be final on giving, birth control, the bringing up of a family, personal habits, tithing, entertainment, buying, selling and other such important matters?

What theological school, from the lowly Bible institute up, could continue to operate if it were to make Christ Lord of its every policy? There may be some, and I hope there are, but I believe I am right when I say that most such schools to stay in business are forced to adopt procedures which find no justification in the Bible they profess to teach. So we have this strange anomaly: the authority of Christ is ignored in order to maintain a school to teach among other things the authority of Christ.

The causes back of the decline in our Lord's authority are many. I name only two.

One is the power of custom, precedent and tradition within the older religious groups. These like gravitation affect every particle of religious practice within the group, exerting a steady and constant pressure in one direction. Of course that direction is toward conformity to the status quo. Not Christ but custom is lord in this situation. And the same thing has passed over (possibly to a slightly lesser degree) into the other groups such as the full gospel tabernacles, the holiness churches, the pentecostal and fundamental churches and the many independent and undenominational churches found everywhere throughout the North American continent.

The second cause is the revival of intellectualism among the evangelicals. This, if I sense the situation correctly, is not so much a thirst for learning as a desire for a reputation of being learned. Because of it good men who ought to know better are being put in the position of collaborating with the enemy. I'll explain.

Our evangelical faith (which I believe to be the true faith of Christ and His apostles) is being attacked these days from many different directions. In the Western world the enemy has forsworn violence. He comes against us no more with sword and fagot; he now comes smiling, bearing gifts. He raises his eyes to heaven and swears that he too believes in the faith of our fathers, but his real purpose is to destroy that faith, or at least to modify it to such an extent that it is no longer the supernatural thing it once was. He comes in the name of philosophy or psychology or anthropology, and with sweet reasonableness urges us to rethink our historic position, to be less rigid, more tolerant, more broadly understanding.

He speaks in the sacred jargon of the schools, and many of our half-educated evangelicals run to fawn on him. He tosses academic degrees to the scrambling sons of the prophets as Rockefeller used to toss dimes to the children of the peasants. The evangelicals who, with some justification, have been accused of lacking true scholarship, now grab for these status symbols with shining eyes, and when they get them they are scarcely able to believe their eyes. They walk about in a kind of ecstatic unbelief, much as the soloist of the neighborhood church choir might were she to be invited to sing at La Scala.

For the true Christian the one supreme test for the present soundness and ultimate worth of everything religious must be the place our Lord occupies in it. Is He Lord or symbol? Is He in charge of the project or merely one of the crew? Does He decide things or only help to carry out the plans of others? All religious activities, from the simplest act of an individual Christian to the ponderous and expensive operations of a whole denomination, may be proved by the answer to the question, Is Jesus Christ Lord in this act? Whether our works prove to be wood, hay and stubble or gold and silver and precious stones in that great day will depend upon the right answer to that question.

What, then, are we to do? Each one of us must decide, and there are at least three possible choices. One is to rise up in shocked indignation and accuse me of irresponsible reporting. Another is to nod general agreement with what is written here but take comfort in the fact that there are exceptions and we are among the exceptions. The other is to go down in meek humility and confess that we have grieved the Spirit and dishonored our Lord in failing to give Him the place His Father has given Him as Head and Lord of the Church.

Either the first or the second will but confirm the wrong. The third if carried out to its conclusion can remove the curse. The decisions lies with us.

20

That Incredible Christian

The current effort of so many religious leaders to harmonize Christianity with science, philosophy and every natural and reasonable thing is, I believe, the result of failure to understand Christianity and, judging from what I have heard and read, failure to understand science and philosophy as well.

At the heart of the Christian system lies the cross of Christ with its divine paradox. The power of Christianity appears in its antipathy toward, never in its agreement with, the ways of fallen men. The truth of the cross is revealed in its contradictions. The witness of the church is most effective when she declares rather than explains, for the gospel is addressed not to reason but to faith. What can be proved requires no faith to accept. Faith rests upon the character of God, not upon the demonstrations of laboratory or logic.

The cross stands in bold opposition to the natural man. Its philosophy runs contrary to the processes of the unregenerate mind, so that Paul could say bluntly that the preaching of the cross is to them that perish foolishness. To try to find a common ground between the message of the cross and man's fallen reason is to try the impossible, and if persisted in must result in an impaired reason, a meaningless cross and a powerless Christianity.

But let us bring the whole matter down from the uplands of theory and simply observe the true Christian as he puts into practice the teachings of Christ and His apostles. Note the contradictions:

The Christian believes that in Christ he has died, yet he is more alive than before and he fully expects to live forever. He walks on earth while seated in heaven and though born on earth he finds that after his conversion he is not at home here. Like the nighthawk, which in the air is the essence of grace and beauty but on the ground is awkward and ugly, so the Christian appears at his best in the heavenly places but does not fit well into the ways of the very society into which he was born.

The Christian soon learns that if he would be victorious as a son of heaven among men on earth he must not follow the common pattern of mankind, but rather the contrary. That he may be safe he puts himself in jeopardy; he loses his life to save it and is in danger of losing it if he attempts to preserve it. He goes down to get up. If he refuses to go down he is already down, but when he starts down he is on his way up.

He is strongest when he is weakest and weakest when he is strong. Though poor he has the power to make others rich, but when he becomes rich his ability to enrich others vanishes. He has most after he has given most away and has least when he possesses most.

He may be and often is highest when he feels lowest and most sinless when he is most conscious of sin. He is wisest when he knows that he knows not and knows least when he has acquired the greatest amount of knowledge. He sometimes does most by doing nothing and goes furthest when standing still. In heaviness he manages to rejoice and keeps his heart glad even in sorrow.

The paradoxical character of the Christian is revealed constantly. For instance, he believes that he is saved now, nevertheless he expects to be saved later and looks forward joyfully to future salvation. He fears God but is not afraid of Him. In God's presence he feels overwhelmed and undone, yet there is nowhere he would rather be than in that presence. He knows that he has been cleansed from his sin, yet he is painfully conscious that in his flesh dwells no good thing.

He loves supremely One whom he has never seen, and though himself poor and lowly he talks familiarly with One who is King of all kings and Lord of all lords, and is aware of no incongruity in so doing. He feels that he is in his own right altogether less than nothing, yet he believes without question that he is the apple of God's eye and that for him the Eternal Son became flesh and died on the cross of shame.

The Christian is a citizen of heaven and to that sacred citizenship he acknowledges first allegiance; yet he may love his earthly country with that intensity of devotion that caused John Knox to pray "O God, give me Scotland or I die."

He cheerfully expects before long to enter that bright world above, but he is in no hurry to leave this world and is quite willing to await the summons of his Heavenly Father. And he is unable to understand why the critical unbeliever should condemn him for this; it all seems so natural and right in the circumstances that he sees nothing inconsistent about it.

The cross-carrying Christian, furthermore, is both a confirmed pessimist and an optimist the like of which is to be found nowhere else on earth.

When he looks at the cross he is a pessimist, for he knows that the same judgment that fell on the Lord of glory condemns in that one act all nature and all the world of men. He rejects every human hope out of Christ because he knows that man's noblest effort is only dust building on dust.

Yet he is calmly, restfully optimistic. If the cross condemns the world the resurrection of Christ guarantees the ultimate triumph of good throughout the universe. Through Christ all will be well at last and the Christian waits the consummation. Incredible Christian!

21

What It Means to Accept Christ

A few things, fortunately only a few, are matters of life and death, such as a compass for a sea voyage or a guide for a journey across the desert. To ignore these vital things is not to gamble or take a chance; it is to commit suicide. Here it is: either be right or be dead.

Our relation to Christ is such a matter of life or death and on a much higher plane. The Bible-instructed man knows that Jesus Christ came into the world to save sinners and that men are saved by Christ alone altogether apart from any works of merit.

That much is true and is known, but obviously the death and resurrection of Christ do not automatically save everyone. How does the individual man come into saving relation to Christ? That some do, we know, but that others do not is evident. How is the gulf bridged between redemption objectively provided and salvation subjectively received? How does that which Christ did for me become operative within me? To the question "What must I do to be saved?" we must learn the correct answer. To fail here is not to gamble with our souls; it is to guarantee eternal banishment from the face of God. Here we must be right or be finally lost.

To this anxious question evangelical Christians provide three answers, "Believe on the Lord Jesus Christ," "Receive Christ as your personal Saviour," and "Accept Christ." Two of the answers are drawn almost verbatim from the Scriptures (Acts 16:31, John 1:12), while the third is a kind of paraphrase meant to sum up the other two. They are therefore not three but one.

Being spiritually lazy we naturally tend to gravitate toward the easiest way of settling our religious questions for ourselves and others; hence the formula "Accept Christ" has become a panacea of universal application, and I believe it has been fatal to many. Though undoubtedly an occasional serious-minded penitent may find in it all the instruction he needs to bring him into living contact with Christ, I fear that too many seekers use it as a short cut to the Promised Land, only to find that it has led them instead to "a land of darkness, as darkness itself; and of the shadow of death, without any order, and where the light is as darkness."

The trouble is that the whole "Accept Christ" attitude is likely to be wrong. It shows Christ applying to us rather than us to Him. It makes Him stand hat-in-hand awaiting our verdict on Him, instead of our kneeling with troubled hearts awaiting His verdict on us. It may even permit us to accept Christ by an impulse of mind or emotions, painlessly, at no loss to our ego and no inconvenience to our usual way of life.

For this ineffectual manner of dealing with a vital matter we might imagine some parallels; as if, for instance, Israel in Egypt had "accepted" the blood of the Passover but continued to live in bondage, or the prodigal son had "accepted" his father's forgiveness and stayed on among the swine in the far country. Is it not plain that if accepting Christ is to mean anything there must be moral action that accords with it?

Allowing the expression "Accept Christ" to stand as an honest effort to say in short what could not be so well said any other way, let us see what we mean or should mean when we use it.

To accept Christ is to form an attachment to the Person of our Lord Jesus altogether unique in human experience.

The attachment is intellectual, volitional and emotional. The believer is intellectually convinced that Jesus is both Lord and Christ; he has set his will to follow Him at any cost and soon his heart is enjoying the exquisite sweetness of His fellowship.

This attachment is all-inclusive in that it joyfully accepts Christ for all that He is. There is no craven division of offices whereby we may acknowledge His Saviourhood today and withhold decision on His Lordship till tomorrow. The true believer owns Christ as his All in All without reservation. He includes all of himself, leaving no part of his being unaffected by the revolutionary transaction.

Further, his attachment to Christ is all-exclusive. The Lord becomes to him not one of several rival interests, but the one exclusive attraction forever. He orbits around Christ as the earth around the sun, held in thrall by the magnetism of His love, drawing all his life and light and warmth from Him. In this happy state he is given other interests, it is true, but these are all determined by his relation to his Lord.

That we accept Christ in this all-inclusive, all-exclusive way is a divine imperative. Here faith makes its leap into God through the Person and work of Christ, but it never divides the work from the Person. It believes on the Lord Jesus Christ, the whole Christ without modification or reservation, and thus it receives and enjoys all that He did in His work of redemption, all that He is now doing in heaven for His own and all that He does in and through them.

To accept Christ is to know the meaning of the words "as he is, so are we in this world" (I John 4:17). We accept His friends as our friends, His enemies as our enemies, His ways as our ways, His rejection as our rejection, His cross as our cross, His life as our life and His future as our future.

If this is what we mean when we advise the seeker to accept Christ, we had better explain it to him. He may get into deep spiritual trouble unless we do.

22

The Inadequacy of "Instant Christianity"

It is hardly a matter of wonder that the country that gave the world instant tea and instant coffee should be the one to give it instant Christianity. If these two beverages were not actually invented in the United States, it was certainly here that they received the advertising impetus that has made them known to most of the civilized world. And it cannot be denied that it was American Fundamentalism that brought instant Christianity to the gospel churches.

Ignoring for the moment Romanism, and Liberalism in its various disguises, and focusing our attention upon the great body of evangelical believers, we see at once how deeply the religion of Christ has suffered in the house of its friends. The American genius for getting things done quickly and easily with little concern for quality or permanence has bred a virus that has infected the whole evangelical church in the United States and, through our literature, our evangelists and our missionaries, has spread all over the world.

Instant Christianity came in with the machine age. Men invented machines for two purposes. They wanted to get important work done more quickly and easily than they could do it by hand, and they wanted to get the work over with so they could give their time to pursuits more to their liking, such as loafing or enjoying the pleasures of the world. Instant Christianity now serves the same purposes in religion. It disposes of the past, guarantees the

future and sets the Christian free to follow the more re-
fined lusts of the flesh in all good conscience and with a
minimum of restraint.

By "instant Christianity" I mean the kind found almost
everywhere in gospel circles and which is born of the notion that we may discharge our total obligation to our own
souls by one act of faith, or at most by two, and be re-
lieved thereafter of all anxiety about our spiritual condition that we may discharge our total obligation to our own
and we are permitted to infer from this that there is no
reason to seek to be saints by character. An automatic,
once-for-all quality is present here that is completely out
of mode with the faith of the New Testament.

In this error, as in most others, there lies a certain
amount of truth imperfectly understood. It is true that
conversion to Christ may be and often is sudden. Where
the burden of sin has been heavy the sense of forgiveness
is usually clear and joyful. The delight experienced in forgiveness is equal to the degree of moral repugnance left in
repentance. The true Christian has met God. He knows he
has eternal life and he is likely to know where and when
he received it. And those also who have been filled with
the Holy Spirit subsequent to their regeneration have a
clear-cut experience of being filled. The Spirit is self-an-
nouncing, and the renewed heart has no difficulty identify-
ing His presence as He floods in over the soul.

But the trouble is that we tend to put our trust in our
experiences and as a consequence misread the entire New
Testament. We are constantly being exhorted to make the
decision, to settle the matter now, to get the whole thing
taken care of at once—and those who exhort us are right
in doing so. There are decisions that can be and should be
made once and for all. There are personal matters that can
be settled instantaneously by a determined act of the will
in response to Bible-grounded faith. No one would want
to deny this; certainly not I.

The question before us is, Just how much can be accomplished in that one act of faith? How much yet remains to be done and how far can a single decision take us?

Instant Christianity tends to make the faith act terminal and so smothers the desire for spiritual advance. It fails to understand the true nature of the Christian life, which is not static but dynamic and expanding. It overlooks the fact that a new Christian is a living organism as certainly as a new baby is, and must have nourishment and exercise to assure normal growth. It does not consider that the act of faith in Christ sets up a personal relationship between two intelligent moral beings, God and the reconciled man, and no single encounter between God and a creature made in His image could ever be sufficient to establish an intimate friendship between them.

By trying to pack all of salvation into one experience, or two, the advocates of instant Christianity flaunt the law of development which runs through all nature. They ignore the sanctifying effects of suffering, cross carrying and practical obedience. They pass by the need for spiritual training, the necessity of forming right religious habits and the need to wrestle against the world, the devil and the flesh.

Undue preoccupation with the initial act of believing has created in some a psychology of contentment, or at least of non-expectation. To many it has imparted a mood of disappointment with the Christian faith. God seems too far away, the world is too near, and the flesh too powerful to resist. Others are glad to accept the assurance of automatic blessedness. It relieves them of the need to watch and fight and pray, and sees them free to enjoy this world while waiting for the next.

Instant Christianity is twentieth-century orthodoxy. I wonder whether the man who wrote Philippians 3:7-16 would recognize it as the faith for which he finally died. I am afraid he would not.

23

There Is No Substitute for Theology

We being what we are and all things else being what they are, the most important and profitable study any of us can engage in is without question the study of theology.

That theology probably receives less attention than any other subject tells us nothing about its importance or lack of it. It indicates rather that men are still hiding from the presence of God among the trees of the garden and feel acutely uncomfortable when the matter of their relation to God is brought up. They sense their deep alienation from God and only manage to live at peace with themselves by forgetting that they are not at peace with God.

If there were no God things would be quite otherwise with us. Were there no one to whom we must finally render up account, at least one big load would be gone from our minds. We would only need to live within the law, not too hard a task in most countries, and there would be nothing to fear. But if God indeed created the earth and placed man upon it in a state of moral probation, then the heavy obligation lies upon us to learn the will of God and do it.

It has always seemed to me completely inconsistent that existentialism should deny the existence of God and then proceed to use the language of theism to persuade men to live right. The French writer, Jean-Paul Sartre, for instance, states frankly that he represents atheistic existentialism. "If God does not exist," he says, "we find no values or commands to turn to which legitimize our conduct. So in the bright realm of values, we have no excuse behind us, nor justification before us. We are all alone, with no excuses." Yet in the next paragraph he states bluntly, "Man is responsible for his passion," and further on, "A coward is responsible for his cowardice." And such considerations as these, he says, fill the existentialist with "anguish, forlornness and despair."

It seems to me that such reasoning must assume the truth of everything it seeks to deny. If there were no God there could be no such word as "responsible." No criminal need fear a judge who does not exist; nor would he need to worry about breaking a law that had not been passed. It is the knowledge that the law and the judge do in fact exist that strikes fear to the lawbreaker's heart. There is someone to whom he is accountable; otherwise the concept of responsibility could have no meaning.

It is precisely because God *is,* and because man is made in His image and is accountable to Him, that theology is so critically important. Christian revelation alone has the answer to life's unanswered questions about God and human destiny. To let these authoritative answers lie neglected while we search everywhere else for answers and find none is, it seems to me, nothing less than folly.

No motorist would be excused if he neglected to consult his road map and tried instead to find his way across the country by looking for moss on logs, or by observing the flight of wild bees or watching the movements of the heavenly bodies. If there *were* no map a man *might* find his way by the stars; but for a traveler trying to get home the stars would be a poor substitute for a map.

Without a map the Greeks did an admirable piece of navigating; but the Hebrews possessed the map and so had no need of human philosophy. As one not wholly unacquainted with Greek thought, it is my belief that but one of Isaiah's eloquent chapters or David's inspired psalms contains more real help for mankind than all the output of the finest minds of Greece during the centuries of her glory.

The present neglect of the inspired Scriptures by civilized man is a shame and a scandal; for those same Scriptures tell him all he wants to know, or should want to know, about God, his own soul and human destiny. It is ironic that men will spend vast amounts both of time and of money in an effort to uncover the secrets of their past when their own future is all that should really matter to them.

No man is responsible for his ancestors; and the only past he must account for is the relatively short one he himself has lived here on earth. To learn how I can escape the guilt of sins committed in my brief yesterdays, how I can live free from sin today and enter at last into the blessed presence of God in a happy tomorrow—that is more important to me than anything that can be discovered by the anthropologist. It appears to me to be a strange perversion of interest to gaze backward at the dust when we are equipped to look upward at the glory.

Whatever keeps me from the Bible is my enemy, however harmless it may appear to be. Whatever engages my attention when I should be meditating on God and things eternal does injury to my soul. Let the cares of life crowd out the Scriptures from my mind and I have suffered loss where I can least afford it. Let me accept anything else instead of the Scriptures and I have been cheated and robbed to my eternal confusion.

The secret of life is theological and the key to heaven as well. We learn with difficulty, forget easily and suffer many distractions. Therefore we should set our hearts to study theology. We should preach it from our pulpits, sing it in our hymns, teach it to our children and make it the subject of conversation when we meet with Christian friends.

24

The Importance of Self-Judgment

Hardly anything else reveals so well the fear and uncertainty among men as the length to which they will go to hide their true selves from each other and even from their own eyes.

Almost all men live from childhood to death behind a semiopaque curtain, coming out briefly only when forced by some emotional shock and then retreating as quickly as possible into hiding again. The result of this lifelong dissimulation is that people rarely know their neighbors for what they really are, and worse than that, the camouflage is so successful that they do not know themselves either.

Self-knowledge is so critically important to us in our pursuit of God and His righteousness that we lie under heavy obligation to do immediately whatever is necessary to remove the disguise and permit our real selves to be known. It is one of the supreme tragedies in religion that so many of us think so highly of ourselves when the evidence lies all on the other side; and our self-admiration effectively blocks out any possible effort to discover a remedy for our condition. Only the man who knows he is sick will go to a physician.

Now, our true moral and spiritual state can be disclosed only by the Spirit and the Word. The final judgment of the heart is God's. There is a sense in which we dare not judge each other (Matt. 7:1-5), and in which we should not even try to judge ourselves (I Cor. 4:3). The ultimate judgment belongs to the One whose eyes are like a flame of fire and who sees quite through the deeds and thoughts of men. I am glad to leave the final word with Him.

There is, nevertheless, a place for self-judgment and a real need that we exercise it (I Cor. 11:31, 32). While our self-discovery is not likely to be complete and our self-judgment is almost certain to be biased and imperfect, there is yet every good reason for us to work along with the Holy Spirit in His benign effort to locate us spiritually in order that we may make such amendments as the circumstances demand. That God already knows us thoroughly is certain (Ps. 139:1-6). It remains for us to know ourselves as accurately as possible. For this reason I offer some rules for self-discovery; and if the results are not all we could desire they may be at least better than none at all. We may be known by the following:

1. *What we want most.* We have but to get quiet, recollect our thoughts, wait for the mild excitement within us to subside, and then listen closely for the faint cry of desire. Ask your heart, What would you rather have than anything else in the world? Reject the conventional answer. Insist on the true one, and when you have heard it you will know the kind of person you are.

2. *What we think about most.* The necessities of life compel us to think about many things, but the true test is what we think about *voluntarily.* It is more than likely that our thoughts will cluster about our secret heart treasure, and whatever that is will reveal what we are. "Where your treasure is, there will your heart be also."

3. *How we use our money.* Again we must ignore those matters about which we are not altogether free. We must pay taxes and provide the necessities of life for ourselves and family, if any. That is routine, merely, and tells us little about ourselves. But whatever money is left to do with as we please—that will tell us a great deal indeed.

4. *What we do with our leisure time.* A large share of

our time is already spoken for by the exigencies of civilized living, but we do have some free time. What we do with it is vital. Most people waste it staring at the television, listening to the radio, reading the cheap output of the press or engaging in idle chatter. What I do with mine reveals the kind of man I am.

5. *The company we enjoy.* There is a law of moral attraction that draws every man to the society most like himself. "Being let go, they went to their own company." Where we go when we are free to go where we will is a near-infallible index of character.

6. *Whom and what we admire.* I have long suspected that the great majority of evangelical Christians, while kept somewhat in line by the pressure of group opinion, nevertheless have a boundless, if perforce secret, admiration for the world. We can learn the true state of our minds by examining our unexpressed admirations. Israel often admired, even envied, the pagan nations around them, and so forgot the adoption and the glory and the covenants and the law and the promises and the fathers. Instead of blaming Israel let us look to ourselves.

7. *What we laugh at.* No one with a due regard for the wisdom of God would argue that there is anything wrong with laughter, since humor is a legitimate component of our complex nature. Lacking a sense of humor we fall that much short of healthy humanity.

But the test we are running here is not whether we laugh or not, but what we laugh at. Some things lie outside the field of pure humor. No reverent Christian, for instance, finds death funny, nor birth nor love. No Spirit-filled man can bring himself to laugh at the Holy Scriptures, or the Church which Christ purchased with His own blood, or prayer or righteousness or human grief or pain. And surely no one who has been in the presence of God could ever laugh at a story involving the Deity.

These are a few tests. The wise Christian will find others.

25

Marks of the Spiritual Man

The concept of spirituality varies among different Christian groups. In some circles the highly vocal person who talks religion continually is thought to be very spiritual; others accept noisy exuberance as a mark of spirituality, and in some churches the man who prays first, longest and loudest gets a reputation for being the most spiritual man in the assembly.

Now a vigorous testimony, frequent prayers and loud praise may be entirely consistent with spirituality, but it is important that we understand that they do not in themselves constitute it nor prove that it is present.

True spirituality manifests itself in certain dominant desires. These are ever-present, deep-settled wants sufficiently powerful to motivate and control the life. For convenience let me number them, though I make no effort to decide the order of their importance.

1. First is the desire to be holy rather than happy. The yearning after happiness found so widely among Christians professing a superior degree of sanctity is sufficient proof that such sanctity is not indeed present. The truly spiritual man knows that God will give abundance of joy after we have become able to receive it without injury to our souls, but he does not demand it at once. John Wesley said of the members of one of the early Methodist societies that he doubted that they had been made perfect in love because they came to church to enjoy religion instead

of to learn how they could become holy.

2. A man may be considered spiritual when he wants to see the honor of God advanced through his life even if it means that he himself must suffer temporary dishonor or loss. Such a man prays "Hallowed be Thy name," and silently adds, "at any cost to me, Lord." He lives for God's honor by a kind of spiritual reflex. Every choice involving the glory of God is for him already made before it presents itself. He does not need to debate the matter with his own heart; there is nothing to debate. The glory of God is necessary to him; he gasps for it as a suffocating man gasps for air.

3. The spiritual man wants to carry his cross. Many Christians accept adversity or tribulation with a sigh and call it their cross, forgetting that such things come alike to saint and sinner. The cross is that extra adversity that comes to us as a result of our obedience to Christ. This cross is not forced upon us; we voluntarily take it up with full knowledge of the consequences. We choose to obey Christ and by so doing choose to carry the cross.

Carrying a cross means to be attached to the Person of Christ, committed to the Lordship of Christ and obedient to the commandments of Christ. The man who is so attached, so committed, so obedient is a spiritual man.

4. Again, a Christian is spiritual when he sees everything from God's viewpoint. The ability to weigh all things in the divine scale and place the same value upon them as God does is the mark of a Spirit-filled life.

God looks *at* and *through* at the same time. His gaze does not rest on the surface but penetrates to the true meaning of things. The carnal Christian looks at an object or a situation, but because he does not see through it he is elated or cast down by what he sees. The spiritual man is able to look through things as God looks and think of them as God thinks. He insists on seeing all things as God sees them even if it humbles him and exposes his ignorance to the point of real pain.

5. Another desire of the spiritual man is to die right rather than to live wrong. A sure mark of the mature man of God is his nonchalance about living. The earth-loving, body-conscious Christian looks upon death with numb terror in his heart; but as he goes on to live in the Spirit he becomes increasingly indifferent to the number of his years here below, and at the same time increasingly careful of the kind of life he lives while he is here. He will not purchase a few extra days of life at the cost of compromise or failure. He wants most of all to be right, and he is happy to let God decide how long he shall live. He knows that he can afford to die now that he is in Christ, but he knows that he cannot afford to do wrong, and this knowledge becomes a gyroscope to stabilize his thinking and his acting.

6. The desire to see others advance at his expense is another mark of the spiritual man. He wants to see other Christians above him and is happy when they are promoted and he is overlooked. There is no envy in his heart; when his brethren are honored he is pleased because such is the will of God and that will is his earthly heaven. If God is pleased, he is pleased for that reason, and if it pleases God to exalt another above him he is content to have it so.

7. The spiritual man habitually makes eternity-judgments instead of time-judgments. By faith he rises above the tug of earth and the flow of time and learns to think and feel as one who has already left the world and gone to join the innumerable company of angels and the general assembly and church of the First-born which are written in heaven. Such a man would rather be useful than famous and would rather serve than be served.

And all this must be by the operation of the Holy Spirit within him. No man can become spiritual by himself. Only the free Spirit can make a man spiritual.

Excerpts from
The Root of the Righteous

26

The Root of the Righteous

One marked difference between the faith of our fathers as conceived by the fathers and the same faith as understood and lived by their children is that the fathers were concerned with the root of the matter, while their present-day descendants seem concerned only with the fruit.

This appears in our attitude toward certain great Christian souls whose names are honored among the churches, as, for instance, Augustine and Bernard in earlier times, or Luther and Wesley in times more recent. Today we write the biographies of such as these and celebrate their fruit, but the tendency is to ignore the root out of which the fruit sprang. "The root of the righteous yieldeth fruit," said the wise man in the Proverbs. Our fathers looked well to the root of the tree and were willing to wait with patience for the fruit to appear. We demand the fruit immediately even though the root may be weak and knobby or missing altogether. Impatient Christians today explain away the simple beliefs of the saints of other days and smile off their serious-minded approach to God and sacred things. They were victims of their own limited religious outlook, but great and sturdy souls withal who managed to achieve a satisfying spiritual experience and do a lot of good in the world in spite of their handicaps. So we'll imitate their fruit without accepting their theology or inconveniencing ourselves too greatly by adopting their all-or-nothing attitude toward religion.

So we say (or more likely think without saying), and every voice of wisdom, every datum of religious experience, every law of nature tells us how wrong we are. The bough that breaks off from the tree in a storm may bloom briefly and give to the unthinking passer-by the impression that it is a healthy and fruitful branch, but its tender blossoms will soon perish and the bough itself wither and die. There is no lasting life apart from the root.

Much that passes for Christianity today is the brief bright effort of the severed branch to bring forth its fruit in its season. But the deep laws of life are against it. Preoccupation with appearances and a corresponding neglect of the out-of-sight root of the true spiritual life are prophetic signs which go unheeded. Immediate "results" are all that matter, quick proofs of present success without a thought of next week or next year. Religious pragmatism is running wild among the orthodox. Truth is whatever works. If it gets results it is good. There is but one test for the religious leader: success. Everything is forgiven him except failure.

A tree can weather almost any storm if its root is sound, but when the fig tree which our Lord cursed "dried up from the roots" it immediately "withered away." A church that is soundly rooted cannot be destroyed, but nothing can save a church whose root is dried up. No stimulation, no advertising campaigns, no gifts of money and no beautiful edifice can bring back life to the rootless tree.

With a happy disregard for consistency of metaphor, the Apostle Paul exhorts us to look to our sources. "Rooted and grounded in love," he says in what is obviously a confusion of figure; and again he urges his readers to be "rooted and built up in him," which envisages the Christian both as a tree to be well rooted and as a temple to rise on a solid foundation.

The whole Bible and all the great saints of the past join to tell us the same thing. "Take nothing for granted," they say to us. "Go back to the grass roots. Open your hearts and search the Scriptures. Bear your cross, follow your Lord and pay no heed to the passing religious vogue. The masses are always wrong. In every generation the number of the righteous is small. Be sure you are among them."

"A man shall not be established by wickedness: but the root of the righteous shall not be moved."

27

God Is Easy to Live With

Satan's first attack upon the human race was his sly effort to destroy Eve's confidence in the kindness of God. Unfortunately for her and for us he succeeded too well. From that day, men have had a false conception of God, and it is exactly this that has cut out from under them the ground of righteousness and driven them to reckless and destructive living.

Nothing twists and deforms the soul more than a low or unworthy conception of God. Certain sects, such as the Pharisees, while they held that God was stern and austere, yet managed to maintain a fairly high level of external morality; but their righteousness was only outward. Inwardly they were "whited sepulchres," as our Lord Himself told them. Their wrong conception of God resulted in a wrong idea of worship. To a Pharisee, the service of God was a bondage which he did not love but from which he could not escape without a loss too great to bear. The God of the Pharisee was not a God easy to live with, so his religion became grim and hard and loveless. It had to be so, for our notion of God must always determine the quality of our religion.

Much Christianity since the days of Christ's flesh has also been grim and severe. And the cause has been the same—an unworthy or an inadequate view of God. Instinctively we try to be like our God, and if He is conceived to be stern and exacting, so will we ourselves be.

From a failure properly to understand God comes a world of unhappiness among good Christians even today. The Christian life is thought to be a glum, unrelieved cross-carrying under the eye of a stern Father who expects much and excuses nothing. He is austere, peevish, highly temperamental and extremely hard to please. The kind of life which springs out of such libelous notions must of necessity be but a parody on the true life of Christ.

It is most important to our spiritual welfare that we hold in our minds always a right conception of God. If we think of Him as cold and exacting we shall find it impossible to love Him, and our lives will be ridden with servile fear. If, again, we hold Him to be kind and understanding our whole inner life will mirror that idea.

The truth is that God is the most winsome of all beings and His service one of unspeakable pleasure. He is all love, and those who trust Him need never know anything but that love. He is just, indeed, and He will not condone sin; but through the blood of the everlasting covenant He is able to act toward us exactly as if we had never sinned. Toward the trusting sons of men His mercy will always triumph over justice.

The fellowship of God is delightful beyond all telling. He communes with His redeemed ones in an easy, uninhibited fellowship that is restful and healing to the soul. He is not sensitive nor selfish nor temperamental. What He is today we shall find Him tomorrow and the next day and the next year. He is not hard to please, though He may be hard to satisfy. He expects of us only what He has Himself first supplied. He is quick to mark every simple effort to please Him, and just as quick to overlook imperfections when He knows we meant to do His will. He loves us for ourselves and values our love more than galaxies of new created worlds.

Unfortunately, many Christians cannot get free from their perverted notions of God, and these notions poison their hearts and destroy their inward freedom. These friends serve God grimly, as the elder brother did, doing what is right without enthusiasm and without joy, and seem altogether unable to understand the buoyant, spirited celebration when the prodigal comes home. Their idea of God rules out the possibility of His being happy in His people, and they attribute the singing and shouting to sheer fanaticism. Unhappy souls, these, doomed to go heavily on their melancholy way, grimly determined to do right if the heavens fall and to be on the winning side in the day of judgment.

How good it would be if we could learn that God is easy to live with. He remembers our frame and knows that we are dust. He may sometimes chasten us, it is true, but even this He does with a smile, the proud, tender smile of a Father who is bursting with pleasure over an imperfect but promising son who is coming every day to look more and more like the One whose child he is.

Some of us are religiously jumpy and self-conscious because we know that God sees our every thought and is acquainted with all our ways. We need not be. God is the sum of all patience and the essence of kindly good will. We please Him most, not by frantically trying to make ourselves good, but by throwing ourselves into His arms with all our imperfections, and believing that He understands everything and loves us still.

28

On Receiving Admonition

An odd little passage in the Book of Ecclesiastes speaks of "an old and foolish king, who will no more be admonished."

It is not hard to understand why an old king, especially if he were a foolish one, would feel that he was beyond admonition. After he had for years given orders, he might easily build a self-confident psychology that simply could not entertain the notion that he should take advice from others. His word had long been law, and to him *right* had become synonymous with his will and *wrong* had come to mean anything that ran contrary to his wishes. Soon the idea that there was anyone wise enough or good enough to reprove him would not so much as enter his mind. He had to be a foolish king to let himself get caught in that kind of web, and an old king to give the web time to get so strong that he could not break it and to give him time to get used to it so that he was no longer aware of its existence.

Regardless of the moral process by which he arrived at his hardened state, the bell had already tolled for him. In every particular he was a lost man. His wizened old body still held together to provide a kind of movable tomb to house a soul already dead. Hope had long ago departed. God had left him to his fatal conceit. And soon he would die physically too, and he would die as a fool dieth.

A state of heart that rejected admonition was characteristic of Israel at various periods in her history, and these periods were invariably followed by judgment. When Christ came to the Jews He found them chuck full of that arrogant self-confidence that would not accept reproof. "We be Abraham's seed," they said coldly when He talked to them about their sins and their need of salvation. The common people heard Him and repented, but the Jewish priests had ruled the roost too long to be willing to surrender their privileged position. Like the old king, they had gotten accustomed to being right all the time. To reprove them was to insult them. They were beyond reproof.

Churches and Christian organizations have shown a tendency to fall into the same error that destroyed Israel: inability to receive admonition. After a time of growth and successful labor comes the deadly psychology of self-congratulation. Success itself becomes the cause of later failure. The leaders come to accept themselves as the very chosen of God. They are special objects of the divine favor; their success is proof enough that this is so. They must therefore be right, and anyone who tries to call them to account is instantly written off as an unauthorized meddler who should be ashamed to dare to reprove his betters.

If anyone imagines that we are merely playing with words let him approach at random any religious leader and call attention to the weaknesses and sins in his organization. Such a one will be sure to get the quick brush off, and if he dares to persist he will be confronted with reports and statistics to prove that he is dead wrong and completely out of order. "We be the seed of Abraham" will be the burden of the defense. And who would dare find fault with Abraham's seed?

Those who have already entered the state where they can no longer receive admonition are not likely to profit by this warning. After a man has gone over the precipice there is not much we can do for him; but we can place markers along the way to prevent the next traveler from going over. Here are a few:

1. Don't defend your church or your organization against criticism. If the criticism is false it can do no harm. If it is true you need to hear it and do something about it.

2. Be concerned not with what you have accomplished but over what you might have accomplished if you had followed the Lord completely. It is better to say (and feel), "We are unprofitable servants: we have done that which was our duty to do."

3. When reproved, pay no attention to the source. Do not ask whether it is a friend or an enemy that reproves you. An enemy is often of greater value to you than a friend because he is not influenced by sympathy.

4. Keep your heart open to the correction of the Lord and be ready to receive His chastisement regardless of who holds the whip. The great saints all learned to take a licking gracefully—and that may be one reason why they were great saints.

29

The Great God Entertainment

A German philosopher many years ago said something to the effect that the more a man has in his own heart the less he will require from the outside; excessive need for support from without is proof of the bankruptcy of the inner man.

If this is true (and I believe it is), then the present inordinate attachment to every form of entertainment is evidence that the inner life of modern man is in serious decline. The average man has no central core of moral assurance, no spring within his own breast, no inner strength to place him above the need for repeated psychological shots to give him the courage to go on living. He has become a parasite on the world, drawing his life from his environment, unable to live a day apart from the stimulation which society affords him.

Schleiermacher held that the feeling of dependence lies at the root of all religious worship, and that however high the spiritual life might rise it must always begin with a deep sense of a great need which only God could satisfy. If this sense of need and a feeling of dependence are at the root of natural religion it is not hard to see why the great god Entertainment is so ardently worshiped by so many. For there are millions who cannot live without amusement; life without some form of entertainment for them is simply intolerable; they look forward to the blessed relief afforded by professional entertainers and other forms of psychological narcotics as a dope addict looks to his daily shot of heroin. Without them they could not summon courage to face existence.

No one with common human feeling will object to the simple pleasures of life, nor to such harmless forms of entertainment as may help to relax the nerves and refresh the mind exhausted by toil. Such things if used with discretion may be a blessing along the way. That is one thing. The all-out devotion to entertainment as a major activity for which and by which men live is definitely something else again.

The abuse of a harmless thing is the essence of sin. The growth of the amusement phase of human life to such fantastic proportions is a portent, a threat to the souls of modern men. It has been built into a multimillion dollar racket with greater power over human minds and human character than any other educational influence on earth. And the ominous thing is that its power is almost exclusively evil, rotting the inner life, crowding out the long eternal thoughts which would fill the souls of men if they were but worthy to entertain them. And the whole thing has grown into a veritable religion which holds its devotees with a strange fascination, and a religion, incidentally, against which it is now dangerous to speak.

For centuries the Church stood solidly against every form of worldly entertainment, recognizing it for what it was—a device for wasting time, a refuge from the disturbing voice of conscience, a scheme to divert attention from moral accountability. For this she got herself abused roundly by the sons of this world. But of late she has become tired of the abuse and has given over the struggle. She appears to have decided that if she cannot conquer the great god Entertainment she may as well join forces with him and make what use she can of his powers. So today we have the astonishing spectacle of millions of dollars being poured into the unholy job of providing earthly entertainment for the so-called sons of heaven. Religious entertainment is in many places rapidly crowding out the serious things of God. Many churches these days have become little more than poor theatres where fifth-rate "producers" peddle their shoddy wares with the full approval of evangelical leaders who can even quote a holy text in defense of their delinquency. And hardly a man dares raise his voice against it.

The great god Entertainment amuses his devotees mainly by telling them stories. The love of stories, which is a characteristic of childhood, has taken fast hold of the minds of the retarded saints of our day, so much so that not a few persons manage to make a comfortable living by spinning yarns and serving them up in various disguises to church people. What is natural and beautiful in a child may be shocking when it persists into adulthood, and more so when it appears in the sanctuary and seeks to pass for true religion.

Is it not a strange thing and a wonder that, with the shadow of atomic destruction hanging over the world and with the coming of Christ drawing near, the professed followers of the Lord should be giving themselves up to religious amusements? That in an hour when mature saints are so desperately needed vast numbers of believers should revert to spiritual childhood and clamor for religious toys?

"Remember, O Lord, what is come upon us: consider, and behold our reproach. . . . The crown is fallen from our head: woe unto us, that we have sinned! For this our heart is faint; for these things our eyes are dim." Amen. Amen.

30

Bible Taught or Spirit Taught

It may shock some readers to suggest that there is a difference between being Bible taught and being Spirit taught.
Nevertheless it is so.

It is altogether possible to be instructed in the rudi-
ments of the faith and still have no real understanding of
the whole thing. And it is possible to go on to become ex-
pert in Bible doctrine and not have spiritual illumination,
with the result that a veil remains over the mind, preventing it from apprehending the truth in its spiritual essence.

Most of us are acquainted with churches that teach the
Bible to their children from their tenderest years, give
them long instruction in the catechism, drill them further
in pastor's classes, and still never produce in them a living
Christianity nor a virile godliness. Their members show no
evidence of having passed from death unto life. None of
the earmarks of salvation so plainly indicated in the Scriptures are found among them. Their religious lives are correct and reasonably moral, but wholly mechanical and
altogether lacking in radiance. They wear their faith as
persons in mourning once wore black arm bands to show
their love and respect for the departed.

Such persons cannot be dismissed as hypocrites. Many
of them are pathetically serious about it all. They are simply blind. From lack of the vital Spirit they are forced to
get along with the outward shell of faith, while all the
time their deep hearts are starving for spiritual reality and

they do not know what is wrong with them.

This difference between the religion of creed and the religion of the Spirit is well set forth by the saintly Thomas in a tender little prayer to his Lord: "The children of Israel in time past said unto Moses, 'Speak thou with us, and we will hear: but let not God speak with us, lest we die.' Not so, Lord, not so, I beseech Thee; but rather with the prophet Samuel, I humbly and earnestly entreat, 'Speak, Lord; for thy servant heareth.' Let not Moses speak unto me, nor any of the prophets, but rather do Thou speak, O Lord God, the inspirer, enlightener of all the prophets; for Thou alone without them canst perfectly instruct me, but they without Thee can profit nothing. They indeed may utter words, but they cannot give the Spirit. Most beautifully do they speak, but if Thou be silent, they inflame not the heart. They teach the letter, but Thou openest the sense; they bring forth mysteries, but Thou unlockest the meaning of sealed things. . . . They work only outwardly, but Thou instructest and enlightenest the heart. . . . They cry aloud with words, but Thou impartest understanding to the hearing."

It would be hard to wrap it up better than that. The same thing has been said variously by others; however, the most familiar saying probably is, "The Scriptures, to be understood, must be read with the same Spirit that originally inspired them." No one denies this, but even such a statement will go over the heads of those who hear it unless the Holy Spirit inflames the heart.

The charge often made against us by Liberals, that we are "bibliolaters," is probably not true in the same sense as meant by our detractors; but candor and self-analysis will force us to admit that there is often too much truth in their charge. Among religious persons of unquestioned orthodoxy there is sometimes found a dull dependence upon the letter of the text without the faintest understanding of its spirit. That truth is in its essence spiritual must consantly be kept before our minds if we would know the truth indeed. Jesus Christ is Himself the Truth, and He cannot be confined to mere words even though, as we ardently believe, He has Himself inspired the words. That which is spiritual cannot be shut in by ink or fenced in by type and paper. The best a book can do is to give us the letter of truth. If we ever receive more than this, it must be by the Holy Spirit who gives it.

The great need of the hour among persons spiritually hungry is twofold: First, to know the Scriptures, apart from which no saving truth will be vouchsafed by our Lord; the second, to be enlightened by the Spirit, apart from whom the Scriptures will not be understood.

31

The Cross Is a Radical Thing

The cross of Christ is the most revolutionary thing ever to appear among men.

The cross of old Roman times knew no compromise; it never made concessions. It won all its arguments by killing its opponent and silencing him for good. It spared not Christ, but slew Him the same as the rest. He was alive when they hung Him on that cross and completely dead when they took Him down six hours later. That was the cross the first time it appeared in Christian history.

After Christ was risen from the dead the apostles went out to preach His message, and what they preached was the cross. And wherever they went into the wide world they carried the cross, and the same revolutionary power went with them. The radical message of the cross transformed Saul of Tarsus and changed him from a persecutor of Christians to a tender believer and an apostle of the faith. Its power changed bad men into good ones. It shook off the long bondage of paganism and altered completely the whole moral and mental outlook of the Western world. All this it did and continued to do as long as it was permitted to remain what it had been originally, a cross. Its power departed when it was changed from a thing of death to a thing of beauty. When men made of it a symbol, hung it around their necks as an ornament or made its outline before their faces as a magic sign to ward off evil, then it became at best a weak emblem, at worst a positive fetish. As such it is revered today by millions who know absolutely nothing about its power.

The cross effects its ends by destroying one established pattern, the victim's, and creating another pattern, its own. Thus it always has its way. It wins by defeating its opponent and imposing its will upon him. It always dominates. It never compromises, never dickers nor confers, never surrenders a point for the sake of peace. It cares not for peace; it cares only to end its opposition as fast as possible.

With perfect knowledge of all this Christ said, "If any man will come after me, let him deny himself, and take up his cross, and follow me." So the cross not only brings Christ's life to an end, it ends also the first life, the old life, of every one of His true followers. It destroys the old pattern, the Adam pattern, in the believer's life, and brings it to an end. Then the God who raised Christ from the dead raises the believer and a new life begins.

This, and nothing less, is true Christianity, though we cannot but recognize the sharp divergence of this conception from that held by the rank and file of evangelicals today. But we dare not qualify our position. The cross stands high above the opinions of men and to that cross all opinions must come at last for judgment. A shallow and worldly leadership would modify the cross to please the entertainment-mad saintlings who will have their fun even within the very sanctuary; but to do so is to court spiritual disaster and risk the anger of the Lamb turned Lion.

We must do something about the cross, and one of two things only we can do—flee it or die upon it. And if we should be so foolhardy as to flee we shall by that act put away the faith of our fathers and make of Christianity something other than it is. Then we shall have left only the empty language of salvation; the power will depart with our departure from the true cross.

If we are wise we will do what Jesus did: endure the

cross and despise its shame for the joy that is set before us. To do this is to submit the whole pattern of our lives to be destroyed and built again in the power of an endless life. And we shall find that it is more than poetry, more than sweet hymnody and elevated feeling. The cross will cut into our lives where it hurts worst, sparing neither us nor our carefully cultivated reputations. It will defeat us and bring our selfish lives to an end. Only then can we rise in fulness of life to establish a pattern of living wholly new and free and full of good works.

The changed attitude toward the cross that we see in modern orthodoxy proves not that God has changed, nor that Christ has eased up on His demand that we carry the cross; it means rather that current Christianity has moved away from the standards of the New Testament. So far have we moved indeed that it may take nothing short of a new reformation to restore the cross to its right place in the theology and life of the Church.

Excerpts from
Of God and Men

32

The Report of the Watcher

Were some watcher or holy one from the bright world above to come among us for a time with the power to diagnose the spiritual ills of church people there is one entry which I am quite sure would appear on the vast majority of his reports: *Definite evidence of chronic spiritual lassitude; level of moral enthusiasm extremely low.*

What makes this condition especially significant is that Americans are not naturally an unenthusiastic people. Indeed they have a world-wide reputation for being just the opposite. Visitors to our shores from other countries never cease to marvel at the vigor and energy with which we attack our problems. We live at a fever pitch, and whether we are erecting buildings, laying highways, promoting athletic events, celebrating special days or welcoming returning heroes we always do it with an exaggerated flourish. Our building will be taller, our highway broader, our athletic contest more colorful, our celebration more elaborate and more expensive than would be true anywhere else on earth. We walk faster, drive faster, earn more, spend more and run a higher blood pressure than any other people in the world.

In only one field of human interest are we slow and apathetic: that is the field of personal religion. There for some strange reason our enthusiasm lags. Church people habitually approach the matter of their personal relation to God in a dull, half-hearted way which is altogether out of keeping with their general temperament and wholly inconsistent with the importance of the subject.

It is true that there is a lot of religious activity among us. Interchurch basketball tournaments, religious splash parties followed by devotions, weekend camping trips with a Bible quiz around the fire, Sunday school picnics, building fund drives and ministerial breakfasts are with us in unbelievable numbers, and they are carried on with typical American gusto. It is when we enter the sacred precincts of the heart's personal religion that we suddenly lose all enthusiasm.

So we find this strange and contradictory situation: a world of noisy, headlong religious activity carried on without moral energy or spiritual fervor. In a year's travel among the churches one scarcely finds a believer whose blood count is normal and whose temperature is up to standard. The flush and excitement of the soul in love must be sought in the New Testament or in the biographies of the saints; we look for them in vain among the professed followers of Christ in our day.

Now if there is any reality within the whole sphere of human experience that is by its very nature worthy to challenge the mind, charm the heart and bring the total life to a burning focus, it is the reality that revolves around the Person of Christ. If He is who and what the Christian message declares Him to be, then the thought of Him should be the most exciting, the most stimulating, to enter the human mind. It is not hard to understand how Paul could join wine and the Spirit in one verse: "Be not drunk with wine, wherein is excess; but be filled with the Spirit" (Eph. 5:18). When the Spirit presents Christ to our inner vision it has an exhilarating effect on the soul, much as wine has on the body. The Spirit-filled man may literally dwell in a state of spiritual fervor amounting to a mild and pure inebriation.

God dwells in a state of perpetual enthusiasm. He is delighted with all that is good and lovingly concerned about all that is wrong. He pursues His labors always in a fullness of holy zeal. No wonder the Spirit came at Pentecost as the sound of a rushing mighty wind and sat in tongues of fire on every forehead. In so doing He was acting as one of the Persons of the blessed Godhead.

Whatever else happened at Pentecost, one thing that cannot be missed by the most casual observer was the sudden upsurging of moral enthusiasm. Those first disciples burned with a steady, inward fire. They were enthusiastic to the point of complete abandon.

Dante, on his imaginary journey through hell, came upon a group of lost souls who sighed and moaned continually as they whirled about aimlessly in the dusky air. Virgil, his guide, explained that these were the "wretched people," the "nearly soulless," who while they lived on earth had not moral energy enough to be either good or evil. They had earned neither praise nor blame. And with them and sharing in their punishment were those angels who would take sides neither with God nor Satan. The doom of all of the weak and irresolute crew was to be suspended forever between a hell that despised them and a heaven that would not receive their defiled presence. Not even their names were to be mentioned again in heaven or earth or hell. "Look," said the guide, "and pass on."

Was Dante saying in his own way what our Lord had said long before to the church of Laodicea: "I would thou wert cold or hot. So then because thou art lukewarm, and neither cold nor hot, I will spue thee out of my mouth"?

The low level of moral enthusiasm among us may have a significance far deeper than we are willing to believe.

33

Exposition Must Have Application

Charles G. Finney believed that Bible teaching without moral application could be worse than no teaching at all and could result in positive injury to the hearers. I used to feel that this might be an extreme position, but after years of observation I have come around to it, or to a view almost identical with it.

There is scarcely anything so dull and meaningless as Bible doctrine taught for its own sake. Truth divorced from life is not truth in its Biblical sense, but something else and something less. Theology is a set of facts concerning God, man and the world. These facts may be and often are set forth as values in themselves; and there lies the snare both for the teacher and for the hearer.

The Bible is among other things a book of revealed truth. That is, certain facts are revealed that could not be discovered by the most brilliant mind. These facts are of such a nature as to be past finding out. They were hidden behind a veil, and until certain men who spoke as they were moved by the Holy Ghost took away that veil no mortal man could know them. This lifting of the veil of unknowing from undiscoverable things we call divine revelation.

The Bible, however, is more than a volume of hitherto unknown facts about God, man and the universe. It is a book of exhortation based upon those facts. By far the greater portion of the book is devoted to an urgent effort to persuade people to alter their ways and bring their lives into harmony with the will of God as set forth in its pages.

No man is better for knowing that God in the beginning created the heaven and the earth. The devil knows that, and so did Ahab and Judas Iscariot. No man is better for knowing that God so loved the world of men that He gave His only begotten Son to die for their redemption. In hell there are millions who know that. Theological truth is useless until it is obeyed. The purpose behind all doctrine is to secure moral action.

What is generally overlooked is that truth as set forth in the Christian Scriptures is a moral thing; it is not addressed to the intellect only, but to the will also. It addresses itself to the total man, and its obligations cannot be discharged by grasping it mentally. Truth engages the citadel of the human heart and is not satisfied until it has conquered everything there. The will must come forth and surrender its sword. It must stand at attention to receive orders, and those orders it must joyfully obey. Short of this any knowledge of Christian truth is inadequate and unavailing.

Bible exposition without moral application raises no opposition. It is only when the hearer is made to understand that truth is in conflict with his heart that resistance sets in. As long as people can hear orthodox truth divorced from life they will attend and support churches and institutions without objection. The truth is a lovely song, become sweet by long and tender association; and since it asks nothing but a few dollars, and offers good music, pleasant friendships and a comfortable sense of well-being, it meets with no resistance from the faithful. Much that passes for New Testament Christianity is little more than objective truth sweetened with song and made palatable by religious entertainment.

Probably no other portion of the Scriptures can compare with the Pauline Epistles when it comes to making artificial saints. Peter warned that the unlearned and the unstable would wrest Paul's writings to their own destruction, and we have only to visit the average Bible conference and listen to a few lectures to know what he meant. The ominous thing is that the Pauline doctrines may be taught with complete faithfulness to the letter of the text without making the hearers one whit the better. The teacher may and often does so teach the truth as to leave the hearers without a sense of moral obligation.

One reason for the divorce between truth and life may be lack of the Spirit's illumination. Another surely is the teacher's unwillingness to get himself into trouble. Any man with fair pulpit gifts can get on with the average congregation if he just "feeds" them and lets them alone. Give them plenty of objective truth and never hint that they are wrong and should be set right, and they will be content.

On the other hand, the man who preaches truth and applies it to the lives of his hearers will feel the nails and the thorns. He will lead a hard life, but a glorious one. May God raise up many such prophets. The church needs them badly.

34

Beware the File-Card Mentality

The essence of true religion is spontaneity, the sovereign movings of the Holy Spirit upon and in the free spirit of redeemed men. This has through the years of human history been the hall mark of spiritual excellency, the evidence of reality in a world of unreality.

When religion loses its sovereign character and becomes mere form, this spontaneity is lost also, and in its place come precedent, propriety, system—and the file-card mentality.

Back of the file-card mentality is the belief that spirituality can be organized. Then is introduced into religion those ideas which never belong there—numbers, statistics, the law of averages, and other such natural and human things. And creeping death always follows.

Now a file card is a very harmless little tool and a very useful one for some purposes. It is splendid for keeping attendance records in the Sunday school, and a good mailing list can hardly be managed without it. It is a good thing in its place and deadly out of its place. Its danger comes from the well-known human tendency to depend upon external helps in dealing with internal things.

When the file card begins to direct the Christian's life, it immediately becomes a nuisance and a curse. When it gets out of the file case and into the human heart, woe be unto us; nothing but an internal spiritual revolution can deliver the victim from his fate.

Here's how the file card works when it gets into the Christian life and begins to create mental habits: It divides the Bible into sections fitted to the days of the year, and compels the Christian to read according to rule. No matter what the Holy Spirit may be trying to say to a man, still he goes on reading where the card tells him, dutifully checking it off each day.

Every Spirit-led saint knows that there are times when he is held by an inward pressure to one chapter, or even one verse, for days at a time while he wrestles with God till some truth does its work within him. To leave that present passage to follow a pre-arranged reading schedule is for him wholly impossible. He is in the hand of the free Spirit, and reality is appearing before him to break and humble and lift and liberate and cheer. But only the free soul can know the glory of this. To this the heart bound by system will be forever a stranger.

The slave to the file card soon finds that his prayers lose their freedom and become less spontaneous, less effective. He finds himself concerned over matters that should give him no concern whatever—how much time he spent in prayer yesterday, whether he did or did not cover his prayer list for the day, whether he gets up as early as he used to do or stays up in prayer as late at night. Inevitably the calendar crowds out the Spirit and the face of the clock hides the face of God. Prayer ceases to be the free breath of a ransomed soul and becomes a duty to be fulfilled. And even if under such circumstances he succeeds in making his prayer amount to something, still he is suffering tragic losses and binding upon his soul a yoke from which Christ died to set him free.

The pastor, too, must watch lest he become the victim of the file card. From the road in, it looks like a good idea to work out a system of sermon coverage, mapping out the doctrines of the Bible as a farmer divides his acres, allowing a certain amount of time during the year for sermons on the various Bible truths so that at the end of a given period proper attention will have been given to each one. Theoretically, this should be fine, but it will kill any man who follows it, and it will kill his church as well; and one characteristic of this kind of death is that neither pastor nor people are aware that it has come.

Those responsible for the activities of churches and gospel workers must look out for the file-card snare. It is a deadly thing and works to quench the spontaneous operation of the Spirit. No one need die, no one need lie in patient, suffering prayer in the presence of God while the Holy Spirit imparts His sovereign will to his believing heart. No vision of God, high and lifted up, no shocking exposure of inner uncleanness, no pain of a burning coal upon the lips.

The glory of the gospel is its freedom. The Pharisees, who were slaves, hated Christ because He was free. The battle for spiritual freedom did not end when our Lord had risen from the dead. It still goes on, and in a tragic degree the sons of freedom are losing it. Many who know better are surrendering their liberties with only a token struggle. They find it easier to consult the card than to pray on to a place of spiritual illumination and inward prophetic assurance.

It will indeed be cause for mourning in Zion when the race of free men dies out in the church and the work of God is entrusted wholly to the file-card jockey.

35

The Use and Abuse of Humor

Few things are as useful in the Christian life as a gentle sense of humor and few things are as deadly as a sense of humor out of control.

Many lose the race of life through frivolity. Paul is careful to warn us. He says plainly that the Christian's characteristic mood should not be one of jesting and foolish talking but rather one of thanksgiving (Eph. 5: 1-5). It is significant that in this passage the apostle classifies levity along with uncleanness, covetousness and idolatry.

Now obviously an appreciation of the humorous is not an evil in itself. When God made us He included a sense of humor as a built-in feature, and the normal human being will possess this gift in some degree at least. The source of humor is ability to perceive the incongruous. Things out of focus appear funny to us and may stir within us a feeling of amusement that will break into laughter.

Dictators and fanatics have no sense of humor. Hitler never knew how funny he looked, nor did Mussolini know how ridiculous he sounded as he solemnly mouthed his bombastic phrases. The religious fanatic will look upon situations so comical as to excite uncontrollable mirth in normal persons and see nothing amusing in them. This blind spot in his make-up prevents him from seeing how badly his own life and beliefs are out of focus. And just so far as he is blind to the incongruous he is abnormal; he is not quite as God meant him to be.

Humor is one thing, but frivolity is quite another. Cultivation of a spirit that can take nothing seriously is one of the great curses of society, and within the church it has worked to prevent much spiritual blessing that otherwise would have descended upon us. We have all met those people who will not be serious. They meet everything with a laugh and a funny remark. This is bad enough in the world, but positively intolerable among Christians.

Let us not allow a perverted sense of humor to ruin us. Some things are funny, and we may well laugh sometimes. But sin isn't funny; death isn't funny. There is nothing funny about a world tottering upon the brink of destruction; nothing funny about war and the sight of boys dying in blood upon the field of battle; nothing funny about the millions who perish each year without ever having heard the gospel of love.

It is time that we draw a line between the false and the true, between the things that are incidental and the things that are vital. Lots of things we can afford to let pass with a smile. But when humor takes religion as the object of its fun it is no longer natural—it is sinful and should be denounced for what it is and avoided by everyone who desires to walk with God.

Innumerable lectures have been delivered, songs sung and books written exhorting us to meet life with a grin and to laugh so the world can laugh with us; but let us remember that however jolly we Christians may become, the devil is not fooling. He is cold-faced and serious, and we shall find at last that he was playing for keeps. If we who claim to be followers of the Lamb will not take things seriously, Satan will, and he is wise enough to use our levity to destroy us.

I am not arguing for unnatural solemnity; I see no value in gloom and no harm in a good laugh. My plea is for a great seriousness which will put us in mood with the Son of Man and with the prophets and apostles of the Scriptures. The joy of the Lord can become the music of our hearts and the cheerfulness of the Holy Spirit will tune the harps within us. Then we may attain that moral happiness which is one of the marks of true spirituality, and also escape the evil effects of unseemly humor.

36

Let's Cultivate Simplicity and Solitude

We Christians must simplify our lives or lose untold treasures on earth and in eternity.

Modern civilization is so complex as to make the devotional life all but impossible. It wears us out by multiplying distractions and beats us down by destroying our solitude, where otherwise we might drink and renew our strength before going out to face the world again.

"The thoughtful soul to solitude retires," said the poet of other and quieter times; but where is the solitude to which we can retire today? Science, which has provided men with certain material comforts, has robbed them of their souls by surrounding them with a world hostile to their existence. "Commune with your own heart upon your bed and be still" is a wise and healing counsel, but how can it be followed in this day of the newspaper, the telephone, the radio and the television? These modern playthings, like pet tiger cubs, have grown so large and dangerous that they threaten to devour us all. What was intended to be a blessing has become a positive curse. No spot is now safe from the world's intrusion.

One way the civilized world destroys men is by preventing them from thinking their own thoughts.

Our "vastly improved methods of communication" of which the shortsighted boast so loudly now enable a few men in strategic centers to feed into millions of minds alien thought-stuff, ready-made and predigested. A little effortless assimilation of these borrowed ideas and the average man has done all the thinking he will or can do. This subtle brainwashing goes on day after day and year after year to the eternal injury of the populace—a populace, incidentally, which is willing to pay big money to have the job done, the reason being, I suppose, that it relieves them of the arduous and often frightening task of reaching independent decisions for which they must take responsibility.

There was a time, not too long ago, when a man's home was his castle, a sure retreat to which he might return for quietness and solitude. There "the rains of heaven may blow in, but the king himself cannot enter without permission," said the proud British, and made good on their boast. That was home indeed. It was of such a sacred place the poet sang:

> O, when I am safe in my sylvan home,
> I tread on the pride of Greece and Rome;
> And when I am stretched beneath the pines,
> Where the evening star so holy shines,
> I laugh at the lore and the pride of man,
> At the sophist schools, and the learned clan;
> For what are they all, in their high conceit,
> When man in the bush with God may meet?
>   —Ralph Waldo Emerson in *Good-bye*

While it is scarcely within the scope of the present piece, I cannot refrain from remarking that the most ominous sign of the coming destruction of our country is the passing of the American home. Americans live no longer in homes, but in theaters. The members of many families hardly know each other, and the face of some popular TV star is to many wives as familiar as that of their husbands. Let no one smile. Rather should we weep at the portent. It will do no good to wrap ourselves in the Stars and Stripes for protection. No nation can long endure whose people have sold themselves for bread and circuses. Our fathers sleep soundly, and the harsh bedlam of commercialized noise that engulfs us like something from Dante's Inferno cannot disturb their slumber. They left us a goodly heritage. To preserve that heritage we must have a national character as strong as theirs. And this can be developed only in the Christian home.

The need for solitude and quietness was never greater than it is today. What the world will do about it is their problem. Apparently the masses want it the way it is and the majority of Christians are so completely conformed to this present age that they, too, want things the way they are. They may be annoyed a bit by the clamor and by the goldfish bowl existence they live, but apparently they are not annoyed enough to do anything about it. However, there are a few of God's children who have had enough. They want to relearn the ways of solitude and simplicity and gain the infinite riches of the interior life. They want to discover the blessedness of what Dr. Max Reich called "spiritual aloneness." To such I offer a brief paragraph of counsel.

Retire from the world each day to some private spot, even if it be only the bedroom (for a while I retreated to the furnace room for want of a better place). Stay in the secret place till the surrounding noises begin to fade out of your heart and a sense of God's presence envelops you. Deliberately tune out the unpleasant sounds and come out of your closet determined not to hear them. Listen for the inward Voice till you learn to recognize it. Stop trying to compete with others. Give yourself to God and then be what and who you are without regard to what others think. Reduce your interests to a few. Don't try to know what will be of no service to you. Avoid the digest type of mind—short bits of unrelated facts, cute stories and bright sayings. Learn to pray inwardly every moment. After a while you can do this even while you work. Practice candor, childlike honesty, humility. Pray for a single eye. Read less, but read more of what is important to your inner life. Never let your mind remain scattered for very long. Call home your roving thoughts. Gaze on Christ with the eyes of your soul. Practice spiritual concentration.

All the above is contingent upon a right relation to God through Christ and daily meditation on the Scriptures. Lacking these, nothing will help us; granted these, the discipline recommended will go far to neutralize the evil effects of externalism and to make us acquainted with God and our own souls.

37

The Bible World Is the Real World

When reading the Scriptures the sensitive person is sure to feel the marked difference between the world as the Bible reveals it and the world as conceived by religious people today. And the contrast is not in our favor.

The world as the men and women of the Bible saw it was a personal world, warm, intimate, populated. Their world contained first of all the God who had created it, who still dwelt in it as in a sanctuary and who might be discovered walking among the trees of the garden if the human eyes clear enough to see. And there were also present many beings sent of God to be ministers to them who were the heirs of salvation. They also recognized the presence of sinister forces which it was their duty to oppose and which they might easily conquer by an appeal to God in prayer.

Christians today think of the world in wholly different terms. Science, which has brought us many benefits, has also brought us a world wholly different from that which we see in the Scriptures. Today's world consists of wide and limitless spaces, having here and there at remote distances from each other blind and meaningless bodies controlled only by natural laws from which they can never escape. That world is cold and impersonal and completely without inhabitants except for man, the little shivering ephemeral being that clings to the soil while he rides "round in earth's diurnal course with rocks and stones and trees."

How glorious is the world as men of the Bible knew it!
Jacob saw a ladder set up on the earth with God standing
above it and the angels ascending and descending upon it.
Abraham and Balaam and Manoah and how many others
met the angels of God and conversed with them. Moses
saw God in the bush; Isaiah saw Him high and lifted up
and heard the antiphonal chant filling the temple.

Ezekiel saw a great cloud and fire unfolding itself, and
out of the midst thereof came the likeness of four living
creatures. Angels were present to tell of Jesus' coming
birth and to celebrate that birth when it took place in Beth-
lehem; angels comforted our Lord when He prayed in
Gethsemane; angels are mentioned in some of the inspired
epistles, and the Book of the Revelation is bright with the
presence of strange and beautiful creatures intent upon
the affairs of earth and heaven.

Yes, the true world is a populated world. The blind eyes
of modern Christians cannot see the invisible but that
does not destroy the reality of the spiritual creation. Unbelief has taken from us the comfort of a personal world.
We have accepted the empty and meaningless world of
science as the true one, forgetting that science is valid
only when dealing with material things and can know
nothing about God and spiritual world.

We must have faith; and let us not apologize for it, for
faith is an organ of knowledge and can tell us more about
ultimate reality than all the findings of science. We are not
opposed to science, but we recognize its proper limitations
and refuse to stop where it is compelled to stop. The Bible
tells of another world too fine for the instruments of
scientific research to discover. By faith we engage that
world and make it ours. It is accessible to us through the
blood of the everlasting covenant. If we will believe we
may even now enjoy the presence of God and the ministry
of His heavenly messengers. Only unbelief can rob us of
this royal privilege.

38

Praise in Three Dimensions

Christ is to His people so many wonderful things and brings to them such a wealth of benefits as the mind cannot comprehend nor the heart find words to express.

These treasures are both present and to come. The Spirit of Truth, speaking through Paul, assures us that God has in Christ blessed us with all spiritual blessings. These are ours as sons of the new creation and are made available to us now by the obedience of faith.

Peter, moved by the same Spirit, tells us of an inheritance guaranteed us by the resurrection of Christ, an inheritance incorruptible, undefiled and unfading, reserved in heaven for us.

There is no contradiction here, for one apostle speaks of present benefits and the other of benefits yet to be conferred upon us at the coming of Christ. And both exhaust human speech to celebrate the many blessings which we have already received.

Perhaps it would help us to understand if we thought of ourselves as fish in a vast river, at once enjoying the full flow of the stream, remembering with gratitude the current that has passed and awaiting with joyous anticipation the fullness that is moving on us from upstream. While this is but an imperfect figure of speech, it is quite literally true that we who trust in Christ are borne along by present grace while we remember with thankfulness the goodness we have enjoyed in days past and look forward in happy expectation to the grace and goodness that yet awaits us.

Bernard of Clairvaux speaks somewhere of a "perfume compounded of the remembered benefits of God." Such fragrance is too rare. Every follower of Christ should be redolent of such perfume; for have we not all received more from God's kindness than our imagination could have conceived before we knew Him and discovered for ourselves how rich and how generous He is?

That we have received of His fullness grace for grace no one will deny; but the fragrance comes not from the receiving; it comes from the remembering, which is something quite different indeed. Ten lepers received their health; that was the benefit. One came back to thank his benefactor; that was the perfume. Unremembered benefits, like dead flies, may cause the ointment to give forth a stinking savor.

Remembered blessings, thankfulness for present favors and praise for promised grace blend like myrrh and aloes and cassia to make a rare bouquet for the garments of the saints. With this perfume David also anointed his harp and the hymns of the ages have been sweet with it.

Perhaps it takes a purer faith to praise God for unrealized blessings than for those we once enjoyed or those we now enjoy. Yet many have risen to that sunlit peak, as did Anna Waring when she wrote,

> *Glory to Thee for all the grace*
> *I have not tasted yet . . .*

As we move into deeper personal acquaintance with the Triune God I think our life emphasis will shift from the past and the present to the future. Slowly we will become children of a living hope and sons of a sure tomorrow. Our hearts will be tender with memories of yesterday and our lives sweet with gratitude to God for the sure way we have come; but our eyes will be focused more and more upon the blessed hope of tomorrow.

Much of the Bible is devoted to prediction. Nothing God has yet done for us can compare with all that is written in the sure word of prophecy. And nothing He has done or may yet do for us can compare with *what He is and will be to us.* Perhaps the hymnist had this in mind when she sang.

> *I have a heritage of joy*
> *That yet I must not see;*
> *The hand that bled to make it mine*
> *Is keeping it for me.*

Could that "heritage of joy" be less than the Beatific Vision?

Excerpts from
Man: the Dwelling Place of God

39

Man: The Dwelling Place of God

Deep inside every man there is a private sanctum where dwells the mysterious essence of his being. This far-in reality is that part of a man which is what it is of itself without reference to any other part of the man's complex nature. It is the man's "I Am," a gift from the I AM who created him.

The I AM which is God is underived and self-existent; the "I Am" which is man is derived from God and dependent every moment upon His creative fiat for its continued existence. One is the Creator, high over all, ancient of days, dwelling in light unapproachable. The other is a creature and, though privileged beyond all others, is still but a creature, a pensioner on God's bounty and a suppliant before His throne.

The deep-in human entity of which we speak is called in the Scriptures *the spirit of man*. "For what man knoweth the things of man, save the spirit of man which is in him? even so the things of God knoweth no man, but the Spirit of God" (I Cor. 2:11). As God's self-knowledge lies in the eternal Spirit, so man's self-knowledge is by his own spirit, and his knowledge of God is by the direct impression of the Spirit of God upon the spirit of man.

The importance of all this cannot be overestimated as we think and study and pray. It reveals the essential spirituality of mankind. It denies that man is a creature having a spirit and declares that he is a spirit having a body.

That which makes him a human being is not his body but his spirit, in which the image of God originally lay.

One of the most liberating declarations in the New Testament is this: "The true worshippers shall worship the Father in spirit and in truth: for the Father seeketh such to worship him. God is a Spirit: and they that worship him must worship him in spirit and in truth" (John 4:23, 24). Here the nature of worship is shown to be wholly spiritual. True religion is removed from diet and days, from garments and ceremonies, and placed where it belongs—in the union of the spirit of man with the Spirit of God.

From man's standpoint the most tragic loss suffered in the Fall was the vacating of this inner sanctum by the Spirit of God. At the far-in hidden center of man's being is a bush fitted to be the dwelling place of the Triune God. There God planned to rest and glow with moral and spiritual fire. Man by his sin forfeited this indescribably wonderful privilege and must now dwell there alone. For so intimately private is the place that no creature can intrude; no one can enter but Christ, and He will enter only by the invitation of faith. "Behold, I stand at the door, and knock: if any man hear my voice, and open the door, I will come in to him, and will sup with him, and he with me" (Rev. 3:20).

By the mysterious operation of the Spirit in the new birth, that which is called by Peter "the divine nature" enters the deep-in core of the believer's heart and establishes residence there. "If any man have not the Spirit of Christ, he is none of his," for "the Spirit itself beareth witness with our spirit, that we are the children of God" (Rom. 8:9, 16). Such a one is a true Christian, and only such. Baptism, confirmation, the receiving of the sacraments, church membership—these mean nothing unless the supreme act of God in regeneration also takes place. Religious externals may have a meaning for the God-inhabited soul; for any others they are not only useless but may actually become snares, deceiving them into a false and perilous sense of security.

"Keep thy heart with all diligence" is more than a wise saying; it is a solemn charge laid upon us by the One who cares most about us. To it we should give the most careful heed lest at any time we should let it slip.

40

Why People Find the Bible Difficult

That many persons find the Bible hard to understand will not be denied by those acquainted with the facts. Testimony to the difficulties encountered in Bible reading is too full and too widespread to be dismissed lightly.

In human experience there is usually a complex of causes rather than but one cause for everything, and so it is with the difficulty we run into with the Bible. To the question, Why is the Bible hard to understand? no snap answer can be given; the pert answer is sure to be the wrong one. The problem is multiple instead of singular, and for this reason the effort to find a single solution to it will be disappointing.

In spite of this I venture to give a short answer to the question, and while it is not the whole answer, it is a major one and probably contains within itself most of the answers to what must be an involved and highly complex question. *I believe that we find the Bible difficult because we try to read it as we would read any other book, and it is not the same as any other book.*

The Bible is not addressed to just anybody. Its message is directed to a chosen few. Whether these few are chosen by God in a sovereign act of election or are chosen because they meet certain qualifying conditions, I leave to each one to decide as he may, knowing full well that his decision will be determined by his basic beliefs about such matters as predestination, free will, the eternal decrees and other related doctrines. But whatever may have taken place in eternity, it is obvious what happens in time: Some believe and some do not; some are morally receptive and some are not; some have spiritual capacity and some have not. It is to those who do and are and have that the Bible is addressed. Those who do not and are not and have not will read it in vain.

Right here I expect some readers to enter strenuous objections, and for reasons not hard to find. Christianity today is man-centered, not God-centered. God is made to wait patiently, even respectfully, on the whims of men. The image of God currently popular is that of a distracted Father, struggling in heartbroken desperation to get people to accept a Saviour of whom they feel no need and in whom they have very little interest. To persuade these self-suff
sufficent souls to respond to His generous offers, God will do almost anything, even using salesmanship methods and talking down to them in the chummiest way imaginable. This view of things is, of course, a kind of religious romanticism which, while it often uses flattering and sometimes embarrassing terms in praise of God, manages nevertheless to make man the star of the show.

The notion that the Bible is addressed to everybody has wrought confusion within and without the church. The effort to apply the teaching of the Sermon on the Mount to the unregenerate nations of the world is one example of this. Courts of law and the military powers of the earth are urged to follow the teachings of Christ, an obviously impossible thing for them to do. To quote the words of Christ as guides for policemen, judges and generals is to misunderstand those words completely and to reveal a total lack of understanding of the purposes of divine revelation. The gracious words of Christ are for the sons and daughters of grace, not for the Gentile nations whose chosen symbols are the lion, the eagle, the dragon and the bear.

Not only does God address His words of truth to those

who are able to receive them, He actually conceals their meaning from those who are not. The preacher uses stories to make truth clear; our Lord often used them to obscure it. The parables of Christ were the exact opposite of the modern "illustration," which is meant to give light; the parables were "dark sayings" and Christ asserted that He sometimes used them so that His disciples could understand and His enemies could not. (See Matthew 13:10-17.) As the pillar of fire gave light to Israel but was cloud and darkness to the Egyptians, so our Lord's words shine in the hearts of His people but leave the self-confident unbeliever in the obscurity of moral night.

The saving power of the Word is reserved for whom it is intended. The secret of the Lord is with them that fear Him. The impenitent heart will find the Bible but a skeleton of facts without flesh or life or breath. Shakespeare may be enjoyed without penitence; we may understand Plato without believing a word he says; but penitence and humility along with faith and obedience are necessary to a right understanding of the Scriptures.

In natural matters faith follows evidence and is impossible without it, but in the realm of the spirit faith precedes understanding; it does not follow it. The natural man must know in order to believe; the spiritual man must believe in order to know. The faith that saves is not a conclusion drawn from evidence; it is a moral thing, a thing of the spirit, a supernatural infusion of confidence in Jesus Christ, a very gift of God.

The faith that saves reposes in the Person of Christ; it leads at once to a committal of the total being to Christ, an act impossible to the natural man. To believe rightly is as much a miracle as was the coming forth of dead Lazarus at the command of Christ.

The Bible is a supernatural book and can be understood only by supernatural aid.

41

Faith: The Misunderstood Doctrine

In the divine scheme of salvation the doctrine of faith is central. God addresses His words to faith, and where no faith is, no true revelation is possible. "Without faith it is impossible to please him."

Every benefit flowing from the atonement of Christ comes to the individual through the gateway of faith. Forgiveness, cleansing, regeneration, the Holy Spirit, all answers to prayer, are given to faith and received by faith. There is no other way. This is common evangelical doctrine and is accepted wherever the cross of Christ is understood.

Because faith is so vital to all our hopes, so necessary to the fulfillment of every aspiration of our hearts, we dare take nothing for granted concerning it. Anything that carries with it so much of weal or woe, which indeed decides our heaven or our hell, is too important to neglect. We simply must not allow ourselves to be uninformed or misinformed. We must know.

For a number of years my heart has been troubled over the doctrine of faith as it is received and taught among evangelical Christians everywhere. Great emphasis is laid upon faith in orthodox circles, and that is good; but still I am troubled. Specifically, my fear is that the modern conception of faith is not the Biblical one; that when the teachers of our day use the word they do not mean what Bible writers meant when they used it.

The causes of my uneasiness are these:

1. The lack of spiritual fruit in the lives of so many who claim to have faith.

2. The rarity of a radical change in the conduct and general outlook of persons professing their new faith in Christ as their personal Saviour.

3. The failure of our teachers to define or even describe the thing to which the word *faith* is supposed to refer.

4. The heartbreaking failure of multitudes of seekers, be they ever so earnest, to make anything out of the doctrine or to receive any satisfying experience through it.

5. The real danger that a doctrine that is parroted so widely and received so uncritically by so many is false as understood by them.

6. I have seen faith put forward as a substitute for obedience, an escape from reality, a refuge from the necessity of hard thinking, a hiding place for weak character. I have known people to miscall by the name of faith high animal spirits, natural optimism, emotional thrills and nervous tics.

7. Plain horse sense ought to tell us that anything that makes no change in the man who professes it makes no difference to God either, and it is an easily observable fact that for countless numbers of persons the change from no-faith to faith makes no actual difference in the life.

Perhaps it will help us to know what faith is if we first notice what it is not. It is not the believing of a statement we know to be true. The human mind is so constructed that it must of necessity believe when the evidence presented to it is convincing. It cannot help itself. When the evidence fails to convince, no faith is possible. No threats, no punishment, can compel the mind to believe against clear evidence.

Faith based upon reason is faith of a kind, it is true; *but it is not of the character of Bible faith*, for it follows the evidence infallibly and has nothing of a moral or spiritual nature in it. Neither can the absence of faith based upon reason be held against anyone, for the evidence, not the individual, decides the verdict. To send a man to hell whose only crime was to follow evidence straight to its proper conclusion would be palpable injustice; to justify a sinner on the grounds that he had made up his mind according to the plain facts would be to make salvation the result of the workings of a common law of the mind as applicable to Judas as to Paul. It would take salvation out of the realm of the volitional and place it in the mental, where, according to the Scriptures, it surely does not belong.

True faith rests upon the character of God and asks no further proof than the moral perfections of the One who cannot lie. It is enough that God said it, and if the statement should contradict every one of the five senses and all the conclusions of logic as well, still the believer continues to believe. "Let God be true, but every man a liar," is the language of true faith. Heaven approves such faith because it rises above mere proofs and rests in the bosom of God.

In recent years among certain evangelicals there has arisen a movement designed to prove the truths of Scriptures by appeal to science. Evidence is sought in the natural world to support supernatural revelation. Snowflakes, blood, stones, strange marine creatures, birds and many other natural objects are brought forward as proof that the Bible is true. This is touted as being a great support to faith, the idea being that if a Bible doctrine can be *proved* to be true, faith will spring up and flourish as a consequence.

What these brethren do not see is that the very fact that they feel a necessity to seek proof for the truths of the Scriptures proves something else altogether, namely, their own basic unbelief. When God speaks unbelief asks, "How shall I know that this is true?" I AM THAT I AM is the only grounds for faith. To dig among the rocks or search under the sea for evidence to support the Scriptures is to insult the One who wrote them. Certainly I do not believe that this is done intentionally; but I cannot see how we can escape the conclusion that it is done, nevertheless.

Faith as the Bible knows it is confidence in God and His Son Jesus Christ; it is the response of the soul to the divine character as revealed in the Scriptures; and even this response is impossible apart from the prior inworking of the Holy Spirit. Faith is a gift of God to a penitent soul and has nothing whatsoever to do with the senses or the data they afford. Faith is a miracle; it is the ability God gives to trust His Son, and anything that does not result in action in accord with the will of God is not faith but something else short of it.

Faith and morals are two sides of the same coin. Indeed the very essence of faith is moral. Any professed faith in Christ as personal Saviour that does not bring the life under plenary obedience to Christ as Lord is inadequate and must betray its victim at the last.

The man that believes will obey; failure to obey is convincing proof that there is not true faith present. To attempt the impossible God must give faith or there will be none, and He gives faith to the obedient heart only. Where real repentance is, there is obedience; for repentance is not only sorrow for past failures and sins, it is also a determination to begin now to do the will of God as He reveals it to us.

42

True Religion Is Not Feeling but Willing

One of the puzzling questions likely to turn up sooner or later to vex the seeking Christian is how he can fulfill the scriptural command to love God with all his heart and his neighbor as himself.

The earnest Christian, as he meditates on his sacred obligation to love God and mankind, may experience a sense of frustration gendered by the knowledge that he just cannot seem to work up any emotional thrill over his Lord or his brothers. He wants to, but he cannot. The delightful wells of feeling simply will not flow.

Many honest persons have become discouraged by the absence of religious emotion and concluded that they are not really Christian after all. They conclude that they must have missed the way somewhere back there and their religion is little more than an empty profession. So for a while they belabor themselves for their coldness and finally settle into a state of dull discouragement, hardly knowing what to think. They do believe in God; they do indeed trust Christ as their Saviour, but the love they hoped to feel consistently eludes them. What is the trouble?

The problem is not a light one. A real difficulty is involved, one which may be stated in the form of a question: How can I love by commandment? Of all the emotions of which the soul is capable, love is by far the freest, the most unreasoning, the one least likely to spring up at the call of duty or obligation, and surely the one that will not come at the command of another. No law has ever been passed that can compel one moral being to love another, for by the very nature of it, love must be voluntary. No one can be coerced or frightened into loving anyone. Love just does not come that way. So what are we to do with our Lord's command to love God and our neighbor?

To find our way out of the shadows and into the cheerful sunlight we need only to know that there are two kinds of love: the love of *feeling* and the love of *willing*. The one lies in the emotions, the other in the will. Over the one we may have little control. It comes and goes, rises and falls, flares up and disappears as it chooses, and changes from hot to warm to cool and back to warm again very much as does the weather. Such love was not in the mind of Christ when He told His people to love God and each other. We could as well command a butterfly to light on our shoulder as to attempt to command this whimsical kind of affection to visit our hearts.

The love the Bible enjoins is not the love of feeling; *it is the love of willing, the willed tendency of the heart.* (For these two happy phrases I am indebted to another, a master of the inner life whose pen was only a short time ago stilled by death.)

God never intended that such a being as man should be the plaything of his feelings. The emotional life is a proper and noble part of the total personality, but it is, by its very nature, of secondary importance. *Religion lies in the will, and so does righteousness.* The only good that God recognizes is a willed good; the only valid holiness is a willed holiness.

It should be a cheering thought that before God every man is what he wills to be. The first requirement in conversion is a rectified will. "If any man will," says our Lord, and leaves it there. To meet the requirements of love toward God, the soul need but will to love and the miracle begins to blossom like the budding of Aaron's rod.

The will is the automatic pilot that keeps the soul on course. "Flying is easy," said a friend who flies his own plane. "Just take her up, point her in the direction you want her to go and set the pilot. After that she'll fly herself." While we must not press the figure too far, it is yet blessedly true that the will, not the feelings, determines moral direction.

The root of all evil in human nature is the corruption of the will. The thoughts and intents of the heart are wrong and as a consequence the whole life is wrong. Repentance is primarily a change of moral purpose, a sudden and often violent reversal of the soul's direction. The prodigal son took his first step upward from the pigsty when he said, "I will arise and go to my father." As he had once willed to leave his father's house, now he willed to return. His subsequent action proved his expressed purpose to be sincere. He *did* return.

Someone may infer from the above that we are ruling out the joy of the Lord as a valid part of the Christian life. To avoid that erroneous conclusion I offer this further word of explanation.

To love God with all our heart we must first of all *will* to do so. We should repent our lack of love and determine from this moment on to make God the object of our devotion. We should set our affections on things above and aim our hearts toward Christ and heavenly things. We should read the Scriptures devotionally every day and prayerfully obey them, always firmly *willing* to love God with all our heart and our neighbor as ourself.

If we do these things we may be sure that we shall experience a wonderful change in our whole inward life. We shall soon find to our great delight that our feelings are becoming less erratic and are beginning to move in the direction of the "willed tendency of the heart." Our emotions will become disciplined and directed. We shall begin to taste the "piercing sweetness" of the love of Christ. Our religious affection will begin to mount evenly on steady wings instead of flitting about idly without purpose or intelligent direction. The whole life, like a delicate instrument, will be tuned to sing the praises of Him who loved us and washed us from our sins in His own blood.

But first of all we must will, for the will is master of the heart.

43

The Old Cross and the New

All unannounced and mostly undetected there has come in modern times a new cross into popular evangelical circles. It is like the old cross, but different: the likenesses are superficial; the differences, fundamental.

From this new cross has sprung a new philosophy of the Chrisitan life, and from that new philosophy has come a new evangelical technique—a new type of meeting and a new kind of preaching. This new evangelism employs the same language as the old, but its content is not the same and its emphasis not as before.

The old cross would have no truck with the world. For Adam's proud flesh it meant the end of the journey. It carried into effect the sentence imposed by the law of Sinai. The new cross is not opposed to the human race; rather, it is a friendly pal and, if understood aright, it is the source of oceans of good clean fun and innocent enjoyment. It lets Adam live without interference. His life motivation is unchanged; he still lives for his own pleasure, only now he takes delight in singing choruses and watching religious movies instead of singing bawdy songs and drinking

This article first appeared in *The Alliance Witness* in 1946. It has been printed in virtually every English-speaking country in the world and has been put into tract form by various publishers, including Christian Publications, Inc. It still appears now and then in the religious press.

hard liquor. The accent is still on enjoyment, though the fun is now on a higher plane morally if not intellectually.

The new cross encourages a new and entirely different evangelistic approach. The evangelist does not demand abnegation of the old life before a new life can be received. He preaches not contrasts but similarities. He seeks to key into public interest by showing that Christianity makes no unpleasant demands; rather, it offers the same thing the world does, only on a higher level. Whatever the sin-mad world happens to be clamoring after at the moment is cleverly shown to be the very thing the gospel offers, only the religious product is better.

The new cross does not slay the sinner, it redirects him. It gears him into a cleaner and jollier way of living and saves his self-respect. To the self-assertive it says, "Come and assert yourself for Christ." To the egotist it says, "Come and do your boasting in the Lord." To the thrill-seeker it says, "Come and enjoy the thrill of Christian fellowship." The Christian message is slanted in the direction of the current vogue in order to make it acceptable to the public.

The philosophy back of this kind of thing may be sincere but its sincerity does not save it from being false. It is false because it is blind. It misses completely the whole meaning of the cross.

The old cross is a symbol of death. It stands for the abrupt, violent end of a human being. The man in Roman times who took up his cross and started down the road had already said good-by to his friends. He was not coming back. He was going out to have it ended. The cross made no compromise, modified nothing, spared nothing; it slew all of the man, completely and for good. It did not try to keep on good terms with its victim. It struck cruel and hard, and when it had finished its work, the man was no more.

The race of Adam is under death sentence. There is no commutation and no escape. God cannot approve any of the fruits of sin, however innocent they may appear or beautiful to the eyes of men. God salvages the individual by liquidating him and then raising him again to newness of life.

That evangelism which draws friendly parallels between the ways of God and the ways of men is false to the Bible and cruel to the souls of its hearers. The faith of Christ does not parallel the world, it intersects it. In coming to Christ we do not bring our old life up onto a higher plane; we leave it at the cross. The corn of wheat must fall into the ground and die.

We who preach the gospel must not think of ourselves as public relations agents sent to establish good will between Christ and the world. We must not imagine ourselves commissioned to make Christ acceptable to big business, the press, the world of sports or modern education. We are not diplomats but prophets, and our message is not a compromise but an ultimatum.

God offers life, but not an improved old life. The life He offers is life out of death. It stands always on the far side of the cross. Whoever would possess it must pass under the rod. He must repudiate himself and concur in God's just sentence against him.

What does this mean to the individual, the condemned man who would find life in Christ Jesus? How can this theology be translated into life? Simply, he must repent and believe. He must forsake his sins and then go on to forsake himself. Let him cover nothing, defend nothing, excuse nothing. Let him not seek to make terms with God, but let him bow his head before the stroke of God's stern displeasure and acknowledge himself worthy to die.

Having done this let him gaze with simple trust upon the risen Saviour, and from Him will come life and rebirth and cleansing and power. The cross that ended the earthly life of Jesus now puts an end to the sinner; and the power that raised Christ from the dead now raises him to a new life along with Christ.

To any who may object to this or count it merely a narrow and private view of truth, let me say God has set His hallmark of approval upon this message from Paul's day to the present. Whether stated in these exact words or not, this has been the content of all preaching that has brought life and power to the world through the centuries. The mystics, the reformers, the revivalists have put their emphasis here, and signs and wonders and mighty operations of the Holy Ghost gave witness to God's approval.

Dare we, the heirs of such a legacy of power, tamper with the truth? Dare we with our stubby pencils erase the lines of the blueprint or alter the pattern shown us in the Mount? May God forbid. Let us preach the old cross and we will know the old power.

44

God Must Be Loved for Himself

God being who He is must always be sought for Himself, never as a means toward something else.

Whoever seeks other objects and not God is on his own; he may obtain those objects if he is able, but he will never have God. God is never found accidentally. "Ye shall seek me, and find me, when ye shall search for me with all your heart" (Jer. 29:13).

Whoever seeks God as a means toward desired ends will not find God. The mighty God, the maker of heaven and earth, will not be one of many treasures, not even the chief of all treasures. He will be all in all or He will be nothing. God will not be used. His mercy and grace are infinite and His patient understanding is beyond measure, but He will not aid men in their selfish striving after personal gain. He will not help men to attain ends which, when attained, usurp the place He by every right should hold in their interest and affection.

Yet popular Christianity has as one of its most effective talking points the idea that God exists to help people to get ahead in this world. The God of the poor has become the God of an affluent society. Christ no longer refuses to be a judge or a divider between money-hungry brothers. He can now be persuaded to assist the brother who has accepted Him to get the better of the brother who has not.

A crass example of the modern effort to use God for selfish purposes is the well-known comedian who, after re-

peated failures, promised someone he called God that if
He would help him to make good in the entertainment
world he would repay Him by giving generously to the
care of sick children. Shortly afterward he hit the big time
in the night clubs and on television. He has kept his word
and is raising large sums of money to build children's hos-
pitals. These contributions to charity, he feels, are a small
price to pay for a success in one of the sleaziest fields of
human endeavor.

One might excuse the act of this entertainer as something to be expected of a twentieth-century pagan; but
that multitudes of evangelicals in North America should
actually believe that God had anything to do with the whole
business is not so easily overlooked. This low and false
view of Deity is one major reason for the immense popularity God enjoys these days among well-fed Westerners.

The teaching of the Bible is that God is Himself the end
for which man was created. "Whom have I in heaven but
thee?" cried the psalmist, "and there is none upon earth
that I desire beside thee" (Ps. 73: 25). The first and
greatest commandment is to love God with every power of
our entire being. Where love like that exists there can be
no place for a second object. If we love God as much as
we should, surely we cannot dream of a loved object beyond Him, which He might help us to obtain.

Bernard of Clairvaux begins his radiant little treatise on
the love of God with a question and an answer. The question, Why should we love God? The answer, Because He
is God. He develops the idea further, but for the enlightened heart little more need be said. We should love
God because He is God. Beyond this the angels cannot
think.

Being who He is, God is to be loved for His own sake.
He is the reason for our loving Him, just as He is the reason for His loving us and for every other act He has performed, is performing and will perform world without
end. God's primary reason for everything is His own good

pleasure. The search for secondary reasons is gratuitous and mostly futile. It affords occupation for theologians and adds pages to books on doctrine, but that it ever turns up any true explanations is doubtful.

But it is the nature of God to share. His mighty acts of creation and redemption were done for His good pleasure, but His pleasure extends to all created things. One has but to look at a healthy child at play or listen to the song of a bird at sundown and he will know that God meant His universe to be a joyful one.

Those who have been spiritually enabled to love God for Himself will find a thousand fountains springing up from the rainbow-circled throne and bringing countless treasures which are to be received with reverent thanksgiving as being the overflow of God's love for His children. Each gift is a bonus of grace which, because it was not sought for itself, may be enjoyed without injury to the soul. These include the simple blessings of life, such as health, a home, a family, congenial friends, food, shelter, the pure joys of nature or the more artificial pleasures of music and art.

The effort to find these treasures by direct search apart from God has been the major activity of mankind through the centuries; and this has been man's burden and man's woe. The effort to gain them as the ulterior motive back of accepting Christ may be something new under the sun; but new or old it is an evil that can only bring judgment at last.

God wills that we should love Him for Himself alone with no hidden reasons, trusting Him to be to us all our natures require. Our Lord said all this much better: "Seek ye first the kingdom of God, and his righteousness; and all these things shall be added unto you" (Matt. 6:33).

45

How to Try the Spirits

These are the times that try men's souls. The Spirit has spoken expressly that in the latter times some should depart from the faith, giving heed to seducing spirits and doctrines of demons; speaking lies in hypocrisy; having their conscience seared with a hot iron. Those days are upon us and we cannot escape them; we must triumph in the midst of them, for such is the will of God concerning us.

Strange as it may seem, the danger today is greater for the fervent Christian than for the lukewarm and the self-satisfied. The seeker after God's best things is eager to hear anyone who offers a way by which he can obtain them. He longs for some new experience, some elevated view of truth, some operation of the Spirit that will raise him above the dead level of religious mediocrity he sees all around him, and for this reason he is ready to give a sympathetic ear to the new and the wonderful in religion, particularly if it is presented by someone with an attractive personality and a reputation for superior godliness.

Now our Lord Jesus, that great Shepherd of the sheep, has not left His flock to the mercy of the wolves. He has given us the Scriptures, the Holy Spirit and natural powers of observation, and He expects us to avail ourselves of their help constantly. "Prove all things; hold fast that which is good," said Paul (I Thess. 5:21). "Beloved, believe not every spirit," wrote John, "but try the spirits whether they are of God: because many false prophets are gone out into the world" (I John 4:1). "Beware of false prophets," our Lord warned, "which come to you in sheep's clothing, but inwardly they are ravening wolves" (Matt. 7:15). Then He added the word by which they may be tested, "Ye shall know them by their fruits."

From this it is plain not only that there shall be false spirits abroad, endangering our Christian lives, but that they may be identified and known for what they are. And of course once we become aware of their identity and learn their tricks, their power to harm us is gone. "Surely in vain the net is spread in the sight of any bird" (Prov. 1:17).

It is my intention to set forth here a method by which we may test the spirits and prove all things religious and moral that come to us or are brought or offered to us by anyone. And while dealing with these matters we should keep in mind that not all religious vagaries are the work of Satan. The human mind is capable of plenty of mischief without any help from the devil. Some persons have a positive genius for getting confused, and will mistake illusion for reality in broad daylight with the Bible open before them. Peter had such in mind when he wrote, "Our beloved brother Paul also according to the wisdom given unto him hath written unto you; as also in all his epistles, speaking in them of these things; in which are some things hard to be understood, which they that are unlearned and unstable wrest, as they do also the other scriptures, unto their own destruction" (II Pet. 3:15, 16).

It is unlikely that the confirmed apostles of confusion will read what is written here or that they would profit much if they did; but there are many sensible Christians who have been led astray but are humble enough to admit their mistakes and are now ready to return unto the Shepherd and Bishop of their souls. These may be rescued from false paths. More important still, there are undoubtedly large numbers of persons who have not left the true way but who want a rule by which they can test everything and by which they may prove the quality of Christian teaching and experience as they come in contact with them day after day throughout their busy lives. For such as these I make available here a little secret by which I have tested my own spiritual experiences and religious impulses for many years.

Briefly stated the test is this: This new doctrine, this new religious habit, this new view of truth, this new spiritual experience—*how has it affected my attitude toward and my relation to God, Christ, the Holy Scriptures, self, other Christians, the world and sin.* By this sevenfold test we may prove everything religious and know beyond a doubt whether it is of God or not. By the fruit of the tree we know the kind of tree it is. So we have but to ask about any doctrine or experience, What is this doing to me? and we know immediately whether it is from above or from below.

1. One vital test of all religious experience is how it affects our relation to God, our concept of God and our attitude toward Him.

God being who He is must always be the supreme arbiter of all things religious. The universe came into existence as a medium through which the Creator might show forth His perfections to all moral and intellectual beings: "I am the Lord: that is my name: and my glory will I not give to another" (Isa. 42:8). "Thou art worthy, O Lord, to receive glory and honour and power: for thou hast created all things, and for thy pleasure they are and were created" (Rev. 4:11).

The health and balance of the universe require that God should be magnified in all things. "Great is the Lord, and greatly to be praised; and his greatness is unsearchable." God acts only for His glory and whatever comes from Him must be to His own high honor. Any doctrine, any experience that serves to magnify Him is likely to be inspired by Him. Conversely, anything that veils His glory or makes Him appear less wonderful is sure to be of the flesh or the devil.

The heart of man is like a musical instrument and may be played upon by the Holy Spirit, by an evil spirit or by the spirit of man himself. Religious emotions are very much the same, no matter who the player may be. Many enjoyable feelings may be aroused within the soul by low or even idolatrous worship. The nun who kneels "breathless with adoration" before an image of the Virgin is having a genuine religious experience. She feels love, awe and reverence, all enjoyable emotions, as certainly as if she were adoring God. The mystical experiences of Hindus and Sufis cannot be brushed aside as mere pretense. Neither dare we dismiss the high religious flights of spiritists and other occultists as imagination. These may have and sometimes do have genuine encounters with something or someone beyond themselves. In the same manner Christians are sometimes led into emotional experiences that are beyond their power to comprehend. I have met such and they have inquired eagerly whether or not their experience was of God.

The big test is, What has this done to my relationship to the God and Father of our Lord Jesus Christ? If this new view of truth—this new encounter with spiritual things—has made me love God more, if it has magnified Him in my eyes, if it has purified my concept of His being and caused Him to appear more wonderful than before, then I may conclude that I have not wandered astray into the pleasant but dangerous and forbidden paths of error.

2. The next test is, How has this new experience affected my attitude toward the Lord Jesus Christ? Whatever place present-day religion may give to Christ, God gives Him top place in earth and in heaven. "This is my beloved Son, in whom I am well pleased," spoke the voice of God from heaven concerning our Lord Jesus. Peter, full of the Holy Spirit, declared: "God hath made that same Jesus, whom ye have crucified, both Lord and Christ"

(Acts 2:36). Jesus said of Himself, "I am the way, the truth, and the life: no man cometh unto the Father, but by me." Again Peter said of Him, "Neither is there salvation in any other: for there is none other name under heaven given among men, whereby we must be saved" (Acts 4:12). The whole Book of Hebrews is devoted to the idea that Christ is above all others. He is shown to be above Aaron and Moses, and even the angels are called to fall down and worship Him. Paul says that He is the image of the invisible God, that in Him dwells the fullness of the Godhead bodily and that in all things He must have the preeminence. But time would fail me to tell of the glory accorded Him by prophets, patriarchs, apostles, saints, elders, psalmists, kings and seraphim. He is made unto us wisdom and righteousness and sanctification and redemption. He is our hope, our life, our all and all, now and forevermore.

All this being true, it is clear that He must stand at the center of all true doctrine, all acceptable practice, all genuine Christian experience. Anything that makes Him less than God has declared Him to be is delusion pure and simple and must be rejected, no matter how delightful or how satisfying it may for the time seem to be.

Christ-less Christianity sounds contradictory but it exists as a real phenomenon in our day. Much that is being done in Christ's name is false to Christ in that it is conceived by the flesh, incorporates fleshly methods, and seeks fleshly ends. Christ is mentioned from time to time in the same way and for the same reason that a self-seeking politician mentions Lincoln and the flag, to provide a sacred front for carnal activities and to deceive the simplehearted listeners. *The* giveaway is that Christ is not central: He is not all and in all.

Again, there are psychic experiences that thrill the seeker and lead him to believe that he has indeed met the Lord and been carried to the third heaven; but the true nature of the phenomenon is discovered later when the face of Christ begins to fade from the victim's consciousness and he comes to depend more and more upon emotional jags as a proof of his spirituality.

If on the other hand the new experience tends to make Christ indispensable, if it takes our interest off our feeling and places it in Christ, we are on the right track. Whatever makes Christ dear to us is pretty sure to be from God.

3. Another revealing test of the soundness of religious experience is, How does it affect my attitude toward the Holy Scriptures?

Did this new experience, this new view of truth, spring out of the Word of God itself or was it the result of some stimulus that lay outside the Bible? Tenderhearted Christians often become victims of strong psychological pressure applied intentionally or innocently by someone's personal testimony, or by a colorful story told by a fervent preacher who may speak with prophetic finality but who has not checked his story with the facts nor tested the soundness of his conclusions by the Word of God.

Whatever originates outside the Scriptures should for that very reason be suspect until it can be shown to be in accord with them. If it should be found to be contrary to the Word of revealed truth, no true Christian will accept it as being from God. However high the emotional content, no experience can be proved to be genuine unless we can find chapter and verse authority for it in the Scriptures. "To the word and to the testimony" must always be the last and final proof.

Whatever is new or singular should also be viewed with a lot of caution until it can furnish scriptural proof of its validity. Over the last half-century quite a number of unscriptural notions have gained acceptance among Christians by claiming that they were among the truths that were to be revealed in the last days. To be sure, say the advocates of this latter-daylight theory, Augustine did not know, Luther did not, John Knox, Wesley, Finney and

Spurgeon did not understand this; but greater light has now shined upon God's people and we of these last days have the advantage of fuller revelation. We should not question the new doctrine nor draw back from this advanced experience. The Lord is getting His Bride ready for the marriage supper of the Lamb. We should all yield to this new movement of the Spirit. So they tell us.

The truth is that the Bible does not teach that there will be new light and advanced spiritual experiences in the latter days; *it teaches the exact opposite.* Nothing in Daniel or the New Testament epistles can be tortured into advocating the idea that we of the end of the Christian era shall enjoy light that was not known at its beginning. Beware of any man who claims to be wiser than the apostles or holier than the martyrs of the Early Church. The best way to deal with him is to rise and leave his presence. You cannot help him and he surely cannot help you.

Granted, however, that the Scriptures may not always be clear and that there are differences of interpretation among equally sincere men, this test will furnish all the proof needed of anything religious, viz., What does it do to my love for and appreciation of the Scriptures?

While true power lies not in the letter of the text but in the Spirit that inspired it, we should never underestimate the value of the letter. The text of truth has the same relation to truth as the honeycomb has to honey. One serves as a receptacle for the other. But there the analogy ends. The honey can be removed from the comb, but the Spirit of truth cannot and does not operate apart from the letter of the Holy Scriptures. For this reason a growing acquaintance with the Holy Spirit will always mean an increasing love for the Bible. The Scriptures are in print what Christ is in person. The inspired Word is like a faithful portrait of Christ. But again the figure breaks down. Christ is in the Bible as no one can be in a mere portrait, for the Bible is a book of holy ideas and the eternal Word of the Father can and does dwell in the thought He has Himself inspired. Thoughts are things, and the thoughts of the Holy Scriptures form a lofty temple for the dwelling place of God.

From this it follows naturally that a true lover of God will be also a lover of His Word. Anything that comes to us from the God of the Word will deepen our love for the Word of God. This follows logically, but we have confirmation by a witness vastly more trustworthy than logic, viz., the concerted testimony of a great army of witnesses living and dead. These declare with one voice that their love for the Scriptures intensified as their faith mounted and their obedience became consistent and joyous.

If the new doctrine, the influence of that new teacher, the new emotional experience fills my heart with an avid hunger to meditate in the Scriptures day and night, I have every reason to believe that God has spoken to my soul and that my experience is genuine. Conversely, if my love for the Scriptures has cooled even a little, if my eagerness to eat and drink of the inspired Word has abated by as much as one degree, I should humbly admit that I have missed God's signal somewhere and frankly backtrack until I find the true way once more.

4. Again, we can prove the quality of religious experience by its effect on the self-life.

The Holy Spirit and the fallen human self are diametrically opposed to each other. "The flesh lusteth against the Spirit, and the Spirit against the flesh: and these are contrary the one to the other: so that ye cannot do the things that ye would" (Gal. 5:17). "They that are after the flesh do mind the things of the flesh; but they that are after the Spirit the things of the Spirit. . . . Because the carnal mind is enmity against God: for it is not subject to the law of God, neither indeed can be" (Rom. 8:5, 7).

Before the Spirit of God can work creatively in our hearts He must condemn and slay the "flesh" within us; that is, He must have our full consent to displace our natural self with the Person of Christ. This displacement is carefully explained in Romans 6, 7, and 8. When the seeking Christian has gone through the crucifying experience described in chapters 6 and 7, he enters into the broad, free regions of chapter 8. There, self is dethroned and Christ is enthroned forever.

In the light of this it is not hard to see why the Christian's attitude toward self is such an excellent test of the validity of his religious experiences. Most of the great masters of the deeper life, such as Fenelon, Molinos, John of the Cross, Madame Guyon and a host of others, have warned against pseudo-religious experiences that provide much carnal enjoyment but feed the flesh and puff up the heart with self-love.

A good rule is this: if this experience has served to humble me and make me little and vile in my own eyes, it is of God; but if it has given me a feeling of self-satisfaction, it is false and should be dismissed as emanating from self or the devil. Nothing that comes from God will minister to my pride or self-congratulation. If I am tempted to be complacent and to feel superior because I have had a remarkable vision or an advanced spiritual experience, I should go at once to my knees and repent of the whole thing. I have fallen a victim to the enemy.

5. Our relation to and our attitude toward our fellow Christians is another accurate test of religious experience.

Sometimes an earnest Christian will, after some remarkable spiritual encounter, withdraw himself from his fellow believers and develop a spirit of faultfinding. He may be honestly convinced that his experience is superior, that he is now in an advanced state of grace, and that the hoi polloi in the church where he attends are but a mixed multitude and he alone is a true son of Israel. He may struggle to be patient with these religious worldlings, but his soft language and condescending smile reveal his true opinion of them—and of himself. This is a dangerous state of mind, and the more dangerous because it can justify itself by the facts. The brother *has* had a remarkable experience; he *has* received some wonderful light on the Scriptures; he *has* entered into a joyous land unknown to him before. And it may easily be true that the professed Christians with whom he is acquainted are worldly and dull and without spiritual enthusiasm. It is not that he is mistaken in his facts that proves him to be in error, but that his reaction to the facts is of the flesh. His new spirituality has made him less charitable.

The Lady Julian tells us in her quaint English how true Christian grace affects our attitude toward others: "For of all things the beholding and loving of the Maker maketh the soul to seem less in his own sight, and most filleth him with reverent dread and true meekness; with plenty of charity to his fellow Christians." Any religious experience that fails to deepen our love for our fellow Christians may safely be written off as spurious.

The apostle John makes love for our fellow Christians to be a test of true faith. "My little children, let us not love in word, neither in tongue; but in deed and in truth. And hereby we know that we are of the truth, and shall assure our hearts before him" (I John 3:18, 19). Again he says, "Beloved, let us love one another: for love is of God; and every one that loveth is born of God, and knoweth God. He that loveth not knoweth not God; for God is love" (I John 4:7, 8).

As we grow in grace we grow in love toward all God's people. "Every one that loveth him that begat loveth him also that is begotten of him" (I John 5:1). This means simply that if we love God we will love His children. All true Christian experience will deepen our love for other Christians.

Therefore we conclude that whatever tends to separate us in person or in heart from our fellow Christians is not of God, but is of the flesh or of the devil. And conversely, whatever causes us to love the children of God is likely to be of God. "By this shall all men know that ye are my disciples, if ye have love one to another" (John 13:35).

6. Another certain test of the source of religious experience is this: Note how it affects our relation to and our attitude toward the world.

By "the world" I do not mean, of course, the beautiful order of nature which God has created for the enjoyment of mankind. Neither do I mean the world of lost men in the sense used by our Lord when He said, "God so loved the world, that he gave his only begotten Son, that whosoever believeth in him should not perish, but have everlasting life. For God sent not his Son into the world to condemn the world; but that the world through him might be saved" (John 3:16, 17). Certainly any true touch of God in the soul will deepen our appreciation of the beauties of nature and intensify our love for the lost. I refer here to something else altogether.

Let an apostle say it for us: "All that is in the world, the lust of the flesh, and the lust of the eyes, and the pride of life, is not of the Father, but is of the world. And the world passeth away, and the lust thereof: but he that doeth the will of God abideth for ever" (I John 2:16, 17).

This is the world by which we may test the spirits. It is the world of carnal enjoyments, of godless pleasures, of the pursuit of earthly riches and reputation and sinful happiness. It carries on without Christ, following the counsel of the ungodly and being animated by the prince of the power of the air, the spirit that works in the children of disobedience (Eph. 2:2). Its religion is a form of godliness, without power, which has a name to live but is dead. It is, in short, unregenerate human society romping on its way to hell, the exact opposite of the true Church of God, which is a society of regenerate souls going soberly but joyfully on their way to heaven.

Any real work of God in our heart will tend to unfit us for the world's fellowship. "Love not the world, neither the things that are in the world. If any man love the world, the love of the Father is not in him" (I John 2:15). "Be ye not unequally yoked together with unbelievers: for what fellowship hath righteousness with unrighteousness? and what communion hath light with darkness?" (II Cor. 6:14). It may be stated unequivocally that any spirit that permits compromise with the world is a false spirit. Any religious movement that imitates the world in any of its manifestations is false to the cross of Christ and on the side of the devil—and this regardless of how much purring its leaders may do about "accepting Christ" or "letting God run your business."

7. The last test of the genuineness of Christian experience is what it does to our attitude toward sin.

The operation of grace within the heart of a believing man will turn that heart away from sin and toward holiness. "For the grace of God that bringeth salvation hath appeared to all men, teaching us that, denying ungodliness and worldly lusts, we should live soberly, righteously, and godly, in this present world; looking for that blessed hope, and the glorious appearing of the great God and our Saviour Jesus Christ" (Titus 2:11-13).

I do not see how it could be plainer. The same grace that saves, teaches, and its teaching is both negative and positive. Negatively it teaches us to deny ungodliness and worldly lusts. Positively it teaches us to live soberly, righteously and godly in this present world.

The man of honest heart will find no difficulty here. He has but to check his own bent to discover whether he is concerned about sin in his life more or less since the supposed work of grace was done. Anything that weakens his hatred of sin may be identified immediately as false to the Scriptures, to the Saviour and to his own soul. Whatever makes holiness more attractive and sin more intolerable may be accepted as genuine. "For thou art not a God that hath pleasure in wickedness: neither shall evil dwell with thee. The foolish shall not stand in thy sight: thou hatest all workers of iniquity" (Ps. 5:4,5).

Jesus warned, "There shall arise false Christs, and false prophets, and shall shew great signs and wonders; insomuch that, if it were possible, they should deceive the very elect." These words describe our day too well to be coincidental. In the hope that the "elect" may profit by them I have set forth these tests. The result is in the hand of God.

46

Some Thoughts on Books and Reading

One big problem in many parts of the world today is to learn how to read, and in others it is to find something to read after one has learned. In our favored West we are overwhelmed with printed matter, so the problem here becomes one of selection. We must decide what not to read.

Nearly a century ago Emerson pointed out that if it were possible for a man to begin to read the day he was born and to go on reading without interruption for seventy years, at the end of that time he would have read only enough books to fill a tiny niche in the British Library. Life is so short and the books available to us are so many that no man can possibly be acquainted with more than a fraction of one percent of the books published.

It hardly need be said that most of us are not selective enough in our reading. I have often wondered how many square yards of newsprint pass in front of the eyes of the average civilized man in the course of a year. Surely it must run into several acres; and I am afraid our average reader does not realize a very large crop of his acreage. The best advice I have heard on this topic was given by a Methodist minister. He said, "Always read your newspaper standing up." Henry David Thoreau also had a low view of the daily press. Just before leaving the city for his now-celebrated sojourn on the banks of Walden Pond, a friend asked him if he would like to have a newspaper delivered to his cottage. "No," replied Thoreau, "I have already seen a newspaper."

In our serious reading we are likely to be too greatly influenced by the notion that the chief value of a book is to inform; and if we were talking of textbooks, of course that would be true, but when we speak or write of books we have not textbooks in mind.

The best book is not one that informs merely, but one that stirs the reader up to inform himself. The best writer is one that goes with us through the world of ideas like a friendly guide who walks beside us through the forest pointing out to us a hundred natural wonders we had not noticed before. So we learn from him to see for ourselves and soon we have no need for our guide. If he has done his work well we can go on alone and miss little as we go.

That writer does the most for us who brings to our attention thoughts that lay close to our minds waiting to be acknowledged as our own. Such a man acts as a midwife to assist at the birth of ideas that have been gestating long within our souls, but which without his help might not have been born at all.

There are few emotions so satisfying as the joy that comes from the act of recognition when we see and identify our own thoughts. We have all had teachers who sought to educate us by feeding alien ideas into our minds, ideas for which we felt no spiritual or intellectual kinship. These we dutifully tried to integrate into our total spiritual philosophy but always without success.

In a very real sense no man can teach another; he can only aid him to teach himself. Facts can be transferred from one mind to another as a copy is made from the master tape on a sound recorder. History, science, even theology, may be taught in this way, but it results in a highly artificial kind of learning and seldom has any good effect upon the deep life of the student. What the learner contributes to the learning process is fully as important as anything contributed by the teacher. If nothing is contributed by the learner the results are useless; at best there will be but the artificial creation of another teacher who can repeat the dreary work on someone else, ad infinitum.

Perception of ideas rather than the storing of them should be the aim of education. The mind should be an eye to see with rather than a bin to store facts in. The man who has been taught by the Holy Spirit will be a seer rather than a scholar. The difference is that the scholar sees and the seer sees through; and that is a mighty difference indeed.

The human intellect even in its fallen state is an awsome work of God, but it lies in darkness until it has been illuminated by the Holy Spirit. Our Lord has little good to say of the unilluminated mind, but He revels in the mind that has been renewed and enlightened by grace. He always makes the place of His feet glorious; there is scarcely anything on earth more beautiful than a Spirit-filled mind, certainly nothing more wonderful than an alert and eager mind made incandescent by the presence of the indwelling Christ.

Since what we read in a real sense enters the soul, it is vitally important that we read the best and nothing but the best. I cannot but feel that Christians were better off before there was so much reading matter to choose from. Today we must practice sharp discipline in our reading habits. Every Christian should master the Bible, or at least spend hours and days and years trying. And always he should read his Bible, as George Muller said, "with meditation."

After the Bible the next most valuable book for the Christian is a *good* hymnal. Let any young Christian spend a year prayerfully meditating on the hymns of Watts and Wesley alone and he will become a fine theologian. Then let him read a balanced diet of the Puritans and the Christian mystics. The results will be more wonderful than he could have dreamed.

47

The Saint Must Walk Alone

Most of the world's great souls have been lonely. Loneliness seems to be one price the saint must pay for his saintliness.

In the morning of the world (or should we say, in that strange darkness that came soon after the dawn of man's creation), that pious soul, Enoch, walked with God and was not, for God took him; and while it is not stated in so many words, a fair inference is that Enoch walked a path quite apart from his contemporaries.

Another lonely man was Noah who, of all the antediluvians, found grace in the sight of God; and every shred of evidence points to the aloneness of his life even while surrounded by his people.

Again, Abraham had Sarah and Lot, as well as many servants and herdsmen, but who can read his story and the apostolic comment upon it without sensing instantly that he was a man "whose soul was alike a star and dwelt apart"? As far as we know not one word did God ever speak to him in the company of men. Face down he communed with his God, and the innate dignity of the man forbade that he assume this posture in the presence of others. How sweet and solemn was the scene that night of

---

This chapter was originally written for *Eternity* magazine and is used here with their kind permission.

the sacrifice when he saw the lamps of fire moving between the pieces of offering. There, alone with a horror of great darkness upon him, he heard the voice of God and knew that he was a man marked for divine favor.

Moses also was a man apart. While yet attached to the court of Pharaoh he took long walks alone, and during one of these walks while far removed from the crowds he saw an Egyptian and a Hebrew fighting and came to the rescue of his countryman. After the resultant break with Egypt he dwelt in almost complete seclusion in the desert. There, while he watched his sheep alone, the wonder of the burning bush appeared to him, and later on the peak of Sinai he crouched alone to gaze in fascinated awe at the Presence, partly hidden, partly disclosed, within the cloud and fire.

The prophets of pre-Christian times differed widely from each other, but one mark they bore in common was their enforced loneliness. They loved their people and gloried in the religion of the fathers, but their loyalty to the God of Abraham, Isaac and Jacob, and their zeal for the welfare of the nation of Israel drove them away from the crowd and into long periods of heaviness. "I am become a stranger unto my brethren, and an alien unto my mother's children," cried one and unwittingly spoke for all the rest.

Most revealing of all is the sight of that One of whom Moses and all the prophets did write, treading His lonely way to the cross. His deep loneliness was unrelieved by the presence of the multitudes.

> 'Tis midnight, and on Olive's brow
>   The star is dimmed that lately shone;
> 'Tis midnight; in the garden now,
>   The suffering Saviour prays alone.
>
> 'Tis midnight, and from all removed
>   The Saviour wrestles lone with fears;
> E'en the disciple whom He loved
>   Heeds not his Master's grief and tears.
>   —William B. Tappan

He died alone in the darkness hidden from the sight of mortal man and no one saw Him when He arose triumphant and walked out of the tomb, though many saw Him afterward and bore witness to what they saw. There are some things too sacred for any eye but God's to look upon. The curiosity, the clamor, the well-meant but blundering effort to help can only hinder the waiting soul and make unlikely if not impossible the communication of the secret message of God to the worshiping heart.

Sometimes we react by a kind of religious reflex and repeat dutifully the proper words and phrases even though they fail to express our real feelings and lack the authenticity of personal experience. Right now is such a time. A certain conventional loyalty may lead some who hear this unfamiliar truth expressed for the first time to say brightly, "Oh, I am never lonely. Christ said, 'I will never leave you nor forsake you,' and, 'Lo, I am with you alway.' How can I be lonely when Jesus is with me?"

Now I do not want to reflect on the sincerity of any Christian soul, but this stock testimony is too neat to be real. It is obviously what the speaker thinks *should* be true rather than what he has proved to be true by the test of experience. This cheerful denial of loneliness proves only that the speaker has never walked with God without the support and encouragement afforded him by society. The sense of companionship which he mistakenly attributes to the presence of Christ may and probably does arise from the presence of friendly people. Always remember: you cannot carry a cross in company. Though a man were surrounded by a vast crowd, his cross is his alone and his carrying of it marks him as a man apart. Society has turned against him; otherwise he would have no cross. No one is a friend to the man with a cross. "They all forsook him, and fled."

The pain of loneliness arises from the constitution of our nature. God made us for each other. The desire for human companionship is completely natural and right. The loneliness of the Christian results from his walk with God in an ungodly world, a walk that must often take him away from the fellowship of good Christians as well as from that of the unregenerate world. His God-given instincts cry out for companionship with others of his kind, others who can understand his longings, his aspirations, his absorption in the love of Christ; and because within his circle of friends there are so few who share his inner experiences, he is forced to walk alone. The unsatisfied longings of the prophets for human understanding caused them to cry out in their complaint, and even our Lord Himself suffered in the same way.

The man who has passed on into the divine Presence in actual inner experience will not find many who understand him. A certain amount of social fellowship will of course be his as he mingles with religious persons in the regular activities of the church, but true spiritual fellowship will be hard to find. But he should not expect things to be otherwise. After all he is a stranger and a pilgrim, and the journey he takes is not on his feet but in his heart. He walks with God in the garden of his own soul—and who but God can walk there with him? He is of another spirit from the multitudes that tread the courts of the Lord's house. He has seen that of which they have only heard, and he walks among them somewhat as Zacharias walked after his return from the altar when the people whispered, "He has seen a vision."

The truly spiritual man is indeed something of an oddity. He lives not for himself but to promote the interests of Another. He seeks to persuade people to give all to his Lord and asks no portion or share for himself. He delights not to be honored but to see his Saviour glorified in the eyes of men. His joy is to see his Lord promoted and himself neglected. He finds few who care to talk about that which is the supreme object of his interest, so he is often silent and preoccupied in the midst of noisy religious shoptalk. For this he earns the reputation of being dull and overserious, so he is avoided and the gulf between him and society widens. He searches for friends upon whose garments he can detect the smell of myrrh and aloes and cassia out of the ivory palaces, and finding few or none, he, like Mary of old, keeps these things in his heart.

It is this very loneliness that throws him back upon God. "When my father and my mother forsake me, then the Lord will take me up." His inability to find human companionship drives him to seek in God what he can find nowhere else. He learns in inner solitude what he could not have learned in the crowd—that Christ is All in All, that He is made unto us wisdom, righteousness, sanctification and redemption, that in Him we have and possess life's *summum bonum*.

Two things remain to be said. One, that the lonely man of whom we speak is not a haughty man, nor is he the holier-than-thou, austere saint so bitterly satirized in popular literature. He is likely to feel that he is the least of all men and is sure to blame himself for his very loneliness. He wants to share his feelings with others and to open his heart to some like-minded soul who will understand him, but the spiritual climate around him does not encourage it, so he remains silent and tells his griefs to God alone.

The second thing is that the lonely saint is not the withdrawn man who hardens himself against human suffering and spends his days contemplating the heavens. Just the opposite is true. His loneliness makes him sympathetic to the approach of the brokenhearted and the fallen and the sin-bruised. Because he is detached from the world, he is all the more able to help it. Meister Eckhart taught his followers that if they should find themselves in prayer as it were caught up to the third heaven and happen to remember that a poor widow needed food, they should break off the prayer instantly and go care for the widow. "God will not suffer you to lose anything by it," he told them. "You can take up again in prayer where you left off and the Lord will make it up to you." This is typical of the great mystics and masters of the interior life from Paul to the present day.

The weakness of so many modern Christians is that they feel too much at home in the world. In their effort to achieve restful "adjustment" to unregenerate society they have lost their pilgrim character and become an essential part of the very moral order against which they are sent to protest. The world recognizes them and accepts them for what they are. And this is the saddest thing that can be said about them. They are not lonely, but neither are they saints.

How to Be Filled with the Holy Spirit

48

How to Be Filled with the Holy Spirit

Before we deal with the question of how to be filled with the Holy Spirit, there are some matters which first have to be settled. As believers you have to get them out of the way, and right here is where the difficulty arises. I have been afraid that my listeners might have gotten the idea somewhere that I had a how-to-be-filled-with-the-Spirit-in-five-easy-lessons doctrine, which I could give you. If you have any such vague ideas as that, I can only stand before you and say, "I am sorry"; because it isn't true; I can't give you such a course. There are some things, I say, that you have to get out of the way, settled. One of them is: Before you are filled with the Holy Spirit you must *be sure that you can be filled.*

Satan has opposed the doctrine of the Spirit-filled life about as bitterly as any other doctrine there is. He has confused it, opposed it, surrounded it with false notions and fears. He has blocked every effort of the Church of Christ to receive from the Father her divine and blood-bought patrimony. The Church has tragically neglected this great liberating truth—that there is now for the child of God a full and wonderful and completely satisfying anointing with the Holy Ghost.

So you have to be sure that it is for you. You must be sure that it is God's will for you; that is, that it is part of the total plan, that it is included and embraced within the work of Christ in redemption; that it is, as the old camp-meeting, praying folks used to say, "the purchase of His blood."

I might throw a bracket in here and say that whenever I use the neutral pronoun "it" I am talking about the gift. When I speak directly of the Holy Spirit, I shall use a personal pronoun, *He* or *Him* or *His*, referring to a person, for the Holy Spirit is not an *it*, but the *gift* of the Holy Spirit must necessarily in our English language be called "it."

You must, I say, be satisfied that this is nothing added or extra. The Spirit-filled life is not a special, de luxe edition of Christianity. It is part and parcel of the total plan of God for His people.

You must be satisfied that it is not abnormal. I admit that it is unusual, because there are so few people who walk in the light of it or enjoy it, but it is not abnormal. In a world where everybody was sick, health would be unusual, but it wouldn't be abnormal. This is unusual only because our spiritual lives are so wretchedly sick and so far down from where they should be.

You must be satisfied, again, that there is nothing about the Holy Spirit queer or strange or eerie. I believe it has been the work of the devil to surround the person of the Holy Spirit with an aura of queerness, or strangeness, so that the people of God feel that this Spirit-filled life is a life of being odd and peculiar, of being a bit uncanny.

That is not true, my friend! The devil manufactured that. He hatched it out, the same devil that once said to our ancient mother, "Yea, hath God said," and thus maligned God Almighty. That same devil has maligned the Holy Ghost. There is nothing eerie, nothing queer, nothing contrary to the normal operations of the human heart about the Holy Ghost. He is only the essence of Jesus imparted to believers. You read the four Gospels and see for yourself how wonderfully calm, pure, sane, simple, sweet, natural, and lovable Jesus was. Even philosophers who don't believe in His deity have to admit the lovableness of

His character.

You must be sure of all this to the point of conviction. That is, you must be convinced to a point where you won't try to persuade God.

You don't have to persuade God at all. There is no persuasion necessary. Dr. Simpson used to say, "Being filled with the Spirit is as easy as breathing; you can simply breathe out and breathe in." He wrote a hymn to that effect. I am sorry that it is not a better hymn, because it is wonderful theology.

Unless you have arrived at this place in your listening and thinking and meditating and praying, where you know that the Spirit-filled life is for you, that there is no doubt about it—no book you read or sermon you heard, or tract somebody sent you is bothering you; you are restful about all this; you are convinced that in the blood of Jesus when He died on the cross there was included, as a purchase of that blood, your right to a full, Spirit-filled life—unless you are convinced of that, unless you are convinced that it isn't an added, unusual, extra, de luxe something that you have to go to God and beg and beat your fists on the chair to get, I recommend this to you: I recommend that you don't do anything about it yet except to meditate upon the Scriptures bearing on this truth. Go to the Word of God and to those parts of it which deal with the subject under discussion tonight and meditate upon them; for "faith cometh by hearing, and hearing by the word of God." Real faith springs not out of sermons but out of the Word of God and out of sermons only so far as they are of the Word of God. I recommend that you be calm and confident about this. Don't get excited, don't despond. The darkest hour is just before the dawn. It may be that this moment of discouragement which you are going through is preliminary to a sunburst of new and beautiful living, if you will follow on to know the Lord.

Remember, fear is of the flesh and panic is of the devil. Never fear and never get panicky. When they came to

Jesus nobody except a hypocrite ever needed to fear Him. When a hypocrite came to Jesus He just sliced him to bits and sent him away bleeding from every pore. If they were ready to give up their sin and follow the Lord and they came in simplicity of heart and said, "Lord, what do You want me to do?" The Lord took all the time in the world to talk to them and explain to them and to correct any false impressions or wrong ideas they had. He is the sweetest, most understanding and wonderful Teacher in the world, and He never panics anybody. It is sin that does that. If there is a sense of panic upon your life, it may be because there is sin in that life of yours which you need to get rid of.

Again, before you can be filled with the Spirit you must desire to be filled. Here I meet with a certain amount of puzzlement. Somebody will say, "How is it that you say to us that we must desire to be filled, because you know we desire to be. Haven't we talked to you in person? Haven't we called you on the phone? Aren't we out here tonight to hear the sermon on the Holy Spirit? Isn't this all a comforting indication to you that we are desirous of being filled with the Holy Spirit?"

Not necessarily, and I will explain why. For instance, are you sure that you want to be possessed by a spirit other than your own? Even though that spirit be the pure Spirit of God? even though He be the very gentle essence of the gentle Jesus? even though He be sane and pure and free? even though He be wisdom personified, wisdom Himself, even though He have a healing, precious ointment to distill? even though He be loving as the heart of God? That Spirit, if He ever possesses you, will be the Lord of your Life!

I ask you, Do you want Him to be Lord of your life? That you want His benefits, I know. I take that for granted. But do you want to be possessed by Him? Do you want to hand the keys of your soul over to the Holy Spirit and say, "Lord, from now on I don't even have a key to my own house. I come and go as Thou tellest me"? Are you willing to give the office of your business establishment, your soul, over to the Lord and say to Jesus, "You sit in this chair and handle these telephones and boss the staff and be Lord of this outfit"? That is what I mean. Are you sure you want this? Are you sure that you desire it?

Are you sure that you want your personality to be taken over by One who will expect obedience to the written and living Word? Are you sure that you want your personality to be taken over by One who will not tolerate the self sins? For instance, self-love. You can no more have the Holy Ghost and have self-love than you can have purity and impurity at the same moment in the same place. He will not permit you to indulge self-confidence. Self-love, self-confidence, self-righteousness, self-admiration, self-aggrandizement, and self-pity are under the interdiction of God Almighty, and He cannot send His mighty Spirit to possess the heart where these things are.

Again, I ask you if you desire to have your personality taken over by One who stands in sharp opposition to the world's easy ways? No tolerance of evil, no smiling at crooked jokes, no laughing off things that God hates. The Spirit of God, if He takes over, will bring you into opposition to the world just as Jesus was brought into opposition to it. The world crucified Jesus because they couldn't stand Him! There was something in Him that rebuked them and they hated Him for it and finally crucified Him. The world hates the Holy Ghost as bad as they ever hated Jesus, the One from whom He proceeds. Are you sure, brother? You want His help, yes; you want a lot of His benefits, yes; but are you willing to go with Him in His opposition to the easygoing ways of the world? If you are not, you needn't apply for anything more than you have, because you don't want Him; you only think you do!

Again, are you sure that you need to be filled? Can't you get along the way you are? You have been doing fairly well: You pray, you read your Bible, you give to missions, you enjoy singing hymns, you thank God you don't drink or gamble or attend theaters, that you are honest, that you have prayer at home. You are glad about all this. Can't you get along like that? Are you sure you need any more than that? I want to be fair with you. I want to do what Jesus did. He turned around to them when they were following Him and told them the truth. I don't want to take you in under false pretense. "Are you sure you want to follow Me?" He asked, and a great many turned away. But Peter said, "Lord, to whom shall we go? Thou hast the words of eternal life." And the crowd that wouldn't turn away was the crowd that made history. The crowd that wouldn't turn back was the crowd that was there when the Holy Ghost came and filled all the place where they were sitting. The crowd that turned back never knew what it was all about.

But maybe you feel in your heart that you just can't go on as you are, that the level of spirituality to which you know yourself called is way beyond you. If you feel that there is something that you must have or your heart will never be satisfied, that there are levels of spirituality, mystic deeps and heights of spiritual communion, purity and power that you have never known, that there is fruit which you know you should bear and do not, victory which you know you should have and have not—I would say, "Come on," because God has something for you tonight.

There is a spiritual loneliness, an inner aloneness, an inner place where God brings the seeker, where he is as lonely as if there were not another member of the Church anywhere in the world. Ah, when you come there, there is a darkness of mind, an emptiness of heart, a loneliness of soul, but it is preliminary to the daybreak. *O God, bring us, somehow, to the daybreak!*

Here is how to receive. First, present your body to Him (Rom. 12: 1, 2). God can't fill what He can't have. Now I ask you: Are you ready to present your body with all of its functions and all that it contains—your mind, your personality, your spirit, your love, your ambitions, your all? That is the first thing. That is a simple, easy act— presenting the body. Are you willing to do it?

Now the second thing is to *ask* (Luke 11: 9-11), and I set aside all theological objections to this text. They say that is not for today. Well, why did the Lord leave it in the Bible then? Why didn't He put it somewhere else; why did He put it where I could see it if He didn't want me to believe it? It is all for us, and if the Lord wanted to do it, He could give it without our asking, but He chooses to have us ask. "Ask of me, and I will give thee" is always God's order; so why not ask?

Acts 5:32 tells us the third thing to do. God gives His Holy Spirit to them that obey Him. Are you ready to obey and do what you are asked to do? What would that be? Simply to live by the Scriptures as you understand them. Simple, but revolutionary.

The next thing is, have faith (Gal. 3:2). We receive Him by faith as we receive the Lord in salvation by faith. He comes as a gift of God to us in power. First He comes in some degree and measure when we are converted; other-wise we couldn't be converted. Without Him we couldn't be born again, because we are born of the Spirit. But I am talking about something different now, an advance over that. I am talking about His coming and possessing the full body and mind and life and heart, taking the whole personality over, gently, but directly and bluntly, and mak-ing it His, so that we may become a habitation of God through the Spirit.

So now suppose we sing. Let us sing *The Comforter Has Come*, because He has come. If He hasn't come to your heart in fullness, He will; but He has come to the earth. He is here and ready, when we present our vessel, to fill our vessel if we will ask and believe. Will you do it?

Worship: The Normal Employment of Moral Beings

49

Worship: The Normal Employment of Moral Beings

Why did Christ come? Why was He conceived? Why was He born? Why was He crucified? Why did He rise again? Why is He now at the right hand of the Father.

The answer to all these questions is, "In order that He might make worshipers out of rebels; in order that He might restore us again to the place of worship we knew when we were first created."

Now because we were created to worship, worship is the normal employment of moral beings. It's the normal employment, not something stuck on or added, like listening to a concert or admiring flowers. It is something that is built into human nature. Every glimpse of heaven shows them worshiping; Ezekiel 1:1-5, the creatures out of the fire were worshiping God; Isaiah 6:1-6, we see the Lord high and lifted up and hear the creatures saying, "Holy, holy, holy, is the Lord of hosts"; Revelation 4:8-11, God opens heaven and we see them there worshiping God the Father; and in the fifth chapter, verses 6 to 14, we see them worshiping God the Son.

Worship is a moral imperative. In Luke 19:37-40 the whole multitude of disciples were worshiping the Lord as He came along and some rebuked them. The Lord said, "Don't rebuke them; if they didn't worship Me the stones would cry out."

Now, worship is the missing jewel in modern evangelicalism. We're organized; we work; we have our agendas.

We have almost everything, but there's one thing that the churches, even the gospel churches, do not have: that is the ability to worship. We are not cultivating the art of worship. It's the one shining gem that is lost to the modern church, and I believe that we ought to search for this until we find it.

I think I ought to talk a little more about what worship is and what it would be like if it were in the church. Well, it's an attitude, a state of mind, a sustained act, subject to degrees of perfection and intensity. As soon as He sends the Spirit of His Son into our hearts we say "Abba" and we're worshiping. That's one thing. But it's quite another thing to be worshipers in the full New Testament sense of the word.

Now I say that worship is subject to degrees of perfection and intensity. There have been those who worshiped God to the point where they were in ecstasies of worship. I once saw a man kneel at an altar, taking Communion. Suddenly he broke into holy laughter. This man laughed until he wrapped his arms around himself as if he was afraid he would burst just out of sheer delight in the presence of Almighty God. A few times I have seen other people rapt in an ecstasy of worship where they were carried away with it, and I have also heard some simple-hearted new converts saying "Abba Father." So worship is capable of running from the very simple to the most intense and sublime.

Now what are the factors that you will find present in worship? Let me give you a few of them as I go along. First there is *boundless confidence.* You cannot worship a Being you cannot trust. Confidence is necessary to respect, and respect is necessary to worship. Worship rises or falls in any church altogether depending upon the attitude we take toward God, whether we see God big or whether we see Him little. Most of us see God too small; our God is too little. David said, "O magnify the Lord with me," and "magnify" doesn't mean to make God big. You can't make

God big. But you can *see* Him big.

Worship, I say, rises or falls with our concept of God; that is why I do not believe in these half-converted cowboys who call God the Man Upstairs. I do not think they worship at all because their concept of God is unworthy of God and unworthy of them. And if there is one terrible disease in the Church of Christ, it is that we do not see God as great as He is. We're too familiar with God.

Communion with God is one thing; familiarity with God is quite another thing. I don't even like (and this may hurt some of your feelings—but they'll heal) to hear God called "You." "You" is a colloquial expression. I can call a man "you," but I ought to call God "Thou" and "Thee." Now I know these are old Elizabethan words, but I also know that there are some things too precious to cast lightly away and I think that when we talk to God we ought to use the pure, respectful pronouns.

Also I think we ought not to talk too much about Jesus just as Jesus. I think we ought to remember who He is. "He is thy Lord; and worship thou him." And though He comes down to the lowest point of our need and makes Himself accessible to us as tenderly as a mother to her child, still don't forget that when John saw Him—that John who had lain on His bosom—he fell at His feet as dead.

I've heard all kinds of preachers. I've heard the ignorant boasters; I've heard the dull, dry ones; I've heard the eloquent ones; but the ones who have helped me most were the ones who were awestruck in the presence of the God about whom they spoke. They might have a sense of humor, they might be jovial; but when they talked about God another tone came into their voice altogether; this was something else, something wonderful. I believe we ought to have again the old Biblical concept of God which makes God awful and makes men lie face down and cry, "Holy, holy, holy, Lord God Almighty." That would do more for the church than everything or anything else.

Then there is *admiration*, that is, appreciation of the excellency of God. Man is better qualified to appreciate God than any other creature because he was made in His image and is the only creature who was. This admiration for God grows and grows until it fills the heart with wonder and delight. "In our astonished reverence we confess Thine uncreated loveliness," said the hymn writer. "In our astonished reverence." The God of the modern evangelical rarely astonishes anybody. He manages to stay pretty much within the constitution. Never breaks over our by-laws. He's a very well-behaved God and very denominational and very much one of us, and we ask Him to help us when we're in trouble and look to Him to watch over us when we're asleep. The God of the modern evangelical isn't a God I could have much respect for. But when the Holy Ghost shows us God as He is we admire Him to the point of wonder and delight.

Fascination is another element in true worship. To be filled with moral excitement. To be captivated and charmed and entranced. Excited, not with how big you're getting or how big the offering was. Not with how many people came out to church. But entranced with who God is, and struck with astonished wonder at the inconceivable elevation and magnitude and splendor of Almighty God.

I remember as a young Christian when I got my first awful, wonderful, entrancing vision of God. I was in West Virginia in the woods sitting on a log reading the Scriptures along with an old Irish evangelist by the name of Robert J. Cunningham, now long in heaven. I got up and wandered away to have prayer by myself. I had been reading one of the driest passages imaginable from the Scriptures—where Israel came out of Egypt and God arranged them into a diamond-shaped camp. He put Levi in the middle and Reuben out in front and Benjamin behind. It was a diamond-shaped moving city with a flame of fire in the middle giving light. Suddenly it broke over me; God is a geometrician; He's an artist! When He laid out that city, He laid it out skillfully, diamond-shaped with a plume in the middle, and it suddenly swept over me like a wave of the sea: how beautiful God is and how artistic and how poetic and how musical, and I worshiped God there under that tree all by himself. You know, after that I began to love the old hymns and I have been a lover of the great hymns ever since.

Next is *adoration*, to love God with all the power within us. To love God with fear and wonder and yearning and awe. To yearn for God with great yearning, and to love Him to a point where it is both painful and delightful. At times this will lead us to breathless silence. I think that some of the greatest prayer is prayer where you don't say one single word or ask for anything. Now God does answer and He does give us what we ask for. That's plain; nobody can deny that unless he denies the Scriptures. But that's only one aspect of prayer, and it's not even the important aspect. Sometimes I go to God and say, "God, if Thou dost never answer another prayer while I live on this earth I will still worship Thee as long as I live and in the ages to come for what Thou hast done already." God's already put me so far in debt that if I were to live one million millenniums I couldn't pay Him for what he's done for me.

We go to God as we send a boy to a grocery store with a long written list, "God, give me this, give me this, and give me this," and our gracious God often does give us what we want. But I think God is disappointed because we make Him to be no more than a source of what we want. Even our Lord Jesus is presented too often as "Someone who will meet your need." That's the throbbing heart of modern evangelism. You're in need and Jesus will meet your need. He's the Need-meeter. Well, He is that indeed; but, ah, He's infinitely more than that.

Now when the mental and emotional and spiritual factors that I've spoken to you about are present and, as I've admitted, in varying degrees of intensity, in song, in praise, in prayer and in mental prayer, you are worshiping. Do you know what mental prayer is? I mean by that, do you know what it is to pray continually? Old Brother Lawrence, who wrote *The Practice of the Presence of God*, said, "If I'm washing dishes I do it to the glory of God and if I pick up a straw from the ground I do it to the glory of God. I'm in communion with God all the time." He said, "The rules tell me that I have to take time off to go alone to pray, and I do, but such times do not differ any from my regular communion." He had learned the art of fellowship with God, continuous and unbroken.

I am afraid of the pastor who enters the pulpit as a different person from what he was before. Reverend, you should never think a thought or do a deed or be caught in any situation that you couldn't carry into the pulpit with you without embarrassment. You should never have to be a different man or get a new voice and a new sense of solemnity when you enter the pulpit. You should be able to enter the pulpit with the same spirit and the same sense of reverence that you had just before when you were talking to someone about the common affairs of life. Moses came down from the mount to speak to the people. Woe be to the church when the pastor comes *up to* the pulpit or comes *into* the pulpit! He must come *down* to the pulpit always. Wesley, they said, habitually dwelt with God but came down at times to speak to the people. So should it be with all of us. *Amen.*

Excerpt from
Who Put Jesus on the Cross?

Christian, Do You Downgrade
Yourself Too Much?

50

Christian, Do You Downgrade Yourself too Much?

Looking for that blessed hope, and the glorious appearing of the great God and our Saviour Jesus Christ; Who gave himself for us, that he might redeem us from all iniquity, and purify unto himself a peculiar people, zealous of good works.

—Titus 2:13-14

The people of God, Christians who are living between the two mighty events of Christ's incarnation and His promised second coming, are not living in a vacuum!

It is amazing that segments in the Christian church that deny the possibility of the imminent return of the Lord Jesus accuse those who do believe in His soon coming of sitting around, twiddling their thumbs, looking at the sky, and blankly hoping for the best!

Nothing could be further from the truth. We live in the interim between His two appearances, but we do not live in a vacuum. We have much to do and little time in which to get it done!

Stretch your mind and consider some very apparent facts of our day.

Who are the Christians leaving all to staff the missionary posts around the world? Who are the Christians staying at home and sacrificing in order to support the great evangelical thrust of the Christian gospel everywhere? Those who fervently believe that He is coming.

What kind of churches are busy praying and teaching

and giving, preparing their young people for the ministry and for missionary work? Churches that are responding to Christ's appeal to "occupy until I come!"

Well, in this text Titus has given us Christian doctrine that has validity both in the light of the expected return of Jesus Christ as well as in the face of death.

It is in the record of the early Methodists in England, when there was persecution and testing in every direction, that John Wesley was able to say, "Our people die well!"

In more recent years, I have heard a quotation from a denominational bishop who estimated that only about ten percent of the men and women in the membership of his church body are prepared and spiritually ready to die when their time comes.

I believe you can only die well when you have lived well, from a spiritual point of view. This doctrine of the Christian life and spiritual vitality of the believer as propounded by Titus has full validity in the face of any contingency which awaits us.

Titus quickly identifies Jesus Christ as the Saviour "who gave himself for us," and we can quickly learn the value of any object by the price which people are willing to pay for it. Perhaps I should qualify that—you may not learn the true value, for it is my private opinion that a diamond or other jewelry has no intrinsic value at all.

You may remember the story about the rooster scratching around in the barnyard for kernels of corn. Suddenly he scratched up a beautiful pearl of fabulous price which had been lost years before, but he just pushed it aside and kept on looking for corn. The pearl had no value for the rooster, although it had a great value for those who had set a price upon it.

There are various kinds of markets in the world, and something which has no value for a disinterested person may be considered of great value by the person desiring it and purchasing it.

It is in this sense, then, that we learn how dear and precious we are to Christ by what He was willing to give for us.

I believe many Christians are tempted to downgrade themselves too much. I am not arguing against true humility and my word to you is this: Think as little of yourself as you want to, but always remember that our Lord Jesus Christ thought very highly of you—enough to give Himself for you in death and sacrifice.

If the devil does come to you and whispers that you are no good, don't argue with him. In fact, you may as well admit it, but then remind the devil: "Regardless of what you say about me, I must tell you how the Lord feels about me. He tells me that I am so valuable to Him that He gave Himself for me on the cross!"

So, the value is set by the price paid—and, in our case, the price paid was our Lord Himself!

The end that the Saviour had in view was that He might redeem us from all iniquity, that is, from the power and consequences of iniquity.

We often sing the words of a hymn by Charles Wesley in which the death of our Lord Jesus is described as "the double cure" for sin. I think many people sing the hymn without realizing what Wesley meant by the double cure.

"Be of sin the double cure, Save me from its wrath and power." The wrath of God against sin and then the power of sin in the human life—these both must be cured. Therefore, when He gave Himself for us, He redeemed us with a double cure, delivering us from the consequences of sin and delivering us from the power which sin exercises in human lives.

Now, Titus, in this great nugget of spiritual truth, reminds us that the redemptive Christ performs a purifying work in the people of God.

You will have to agree with me that one of the deep and outbroken diseases of this present world and society is impurity, and it displays itself in dozens of symptoms. We are prone to look upon certain lewd and indecent physical actions as the impurities which plague human life and society—but the actual lusting and scheming and planning and plotting come from a far deeper source of impurity within the very minds and innermost beings of sinful men and women.

If we were people of clean hands and pure hearts, we would be intent upon doing the things that please God. Impurity is not just a wrong action; impurity is the state of mind and heart and soul which is just the opposite of purity and wholeness.

Sexual misconduct is a symptom of the disease of impurity—but so is hatred. Pride and egotism, resentfulness and churlishness come to the surface out of sinful and impure minds and hearts, just as gluttony and slothfulness and self-indulgence do. All of these and countless others come to the surface as outward symptoms of the deep, inward disease of selfishness and sin.

Because this is a fact in life and experience, it is the spiritual work of Jesus Christ to purify His people by His own blood to rid them of this deep-lying disease. That is why He is called the Great Physician—He is able to heal us of this plague of impurity and iniquity, redeeming us from the consequences of our sins and purifying us from the presence of our sins.

Now, brethren, either this is true and realizable in human life and experience or Christianity is the cheap fraud of the day. Either it is true and a dependable spiritual option or we should fold up the Bible and put it away with other classical pieces of literature which have no particular validity in the face of death.

Thank God that there are millions who dare to stand as if in a great chorus and shout with me, "It is true! He did give Himself to redeem us from all iniquity and He does perform this purifying work in our lives day by day!"

The result of Christ's purifying work is the perfecting of God's very own people, referred to in this passage from the King James version as "a peculiar people."

Many of us know all too well that this word *peculiar* has been often used to cloak religious conduct both strange and irrational. People have been known to do rather weird things and then grin a self-conscious grin and say in half-hearted apology: "Well, we are a peculiar people!"

Anyone with a serious and honest concern for scriptural admonition and instruction could quickly learn that this English word *peculiar* in the language of 1611 describing the redeemed people of God had no connotation of queerness, ridiculousness nor foolishness.

The same word was first used in Exodus 19:5 when God said that Israel "shall be unto me a peculiar treasure above all people." It was God's way of emphasizing that His people would be to Him a treasure above all other treasures. In the etymological sense, it means "shut up to me as my special jewel."

Every loving mother and father has a good idea of what God meant. There are babies in houses up and down every street, as you can tell by the baby clothes hanging on the lines of a summer day.

But in the house where you live, there is one little infant in particular, and he is a peculiar treasure unto you above all others. It does not mean necessarily that he is prettier, but it does mean that he is the treasure above all other treasures and you would not trade him for any other child in the whole world. He is a *peculiar* treasure!

This gives us some idea, at least, of what we are—God's special jewels marked out for him!

Titus then clearly spelled out one thing that will always characterize the children of God—the fact that they are zealous of good works.

Titus and all of the other writers who had a part in God's revelation through the scriptures agree at this point—our Lord never made provision for any of His followers to be "armchair" Christians. "Ivory tower" Christianity, an abstract kind of believing, composed simply of fine and beautiful thoughts, is not what Jesus taught at all.

The language in this passage is plain: The children of God in Jesus Christ, redeemed by the giving of Himself, purified and made unto Him as special jewels, a peculiar people, are characterized by one thing—their zeal for good works.

Because of the grace of God, we learn, these followers of Jesus Christ are zealous of good works and in their daily experience they live "looking." The Christian should always live in joyous anticipation of the blessed hope and the glorious appearing of the great God and our Saviour Jesus Christ!

Now, there is something in Christian theology that I want to share with you. Some people say they cannot bother with theology because they do not know either Greek or Hebrew. I cannot believe that there is any Christian who is so humble that he would insist that he knows nothing about theology.

Theology is the study of God and we have a very wonderful textbook—actually 66 textbooks rolled into one. We call it the Bible. The point I want to make is this: I have noted in study and in experience that the more vital and important any theological or doctrinal truth may be, the devil will fight it harder and bring greater controversy to bear upon it.

Consider the deity of Jesus, for example.

More and more people are arguing and debating and fighting over this absolutely vital and foundational truth.

The devil is smart enough not to waste his attacks on minor and nonvital aspects of Christian truth and teaching.

The devil will not cause any trouble for a preacher who is scared stiff of his congregation and worried about his job to the extent that he preaches for thirty minutes and the sum of what he says is "Be good and you will feel better!"

You can be as good as you want to and yet go to hell if

you have not put your trust in Jesus Christ! The devil is not going to waste his time causing any trouble for the preacher whose only message is "Be good!"

But the believing Christian lives in joyful anticipation of the return of Jesus Christ and that is such an important segment of truth that the devil has always been geared up to fight it and ridicule it. One of his big successes is being able to get people to argue and get mad about the second coming—rather than looking and waiting for it.

Suppose a man has been overseas two or three years, away from his family. Suddenly a cable arrives for the family with the message, "My work completed here; I will be home today."

After some hours he arrives at the front door and finds the members of his family in turmoil. There had been a great argument as to whether he would arrive in the afternoon or evening. There had been arguments about what transportation he would be using. As a result, there were no little noses pushing against the window glass, no one looking to be able to catch the first glimpse of returning Daddy.

You may say, "That is only an illustration."

But what is the situation in the various segments of the Christian community?

They are fighting with one another and glaring at each other. They are debating whether He is coming and how He is coming and they are busy using what they consider to be proof texts about the fall of Rome and the identification of the anti-Christ.

Brethren, that is the work of the devil—to make Christian people argue about the details of His coming so they will forget the most important thing. How many Christians are so confused and bewildered by the arguments that they have forgotten that the Saviour has purified unto Himself a peculiar people, expecting that we will live soberly, righteously and godly, looking for the glorious appearing of the great God and Saviour.

That is the Epiphany, which is an expression in the Christian church, and it is used in reference to Christ's manifestation in the world.

It is used in two senses in 1 Timothy and 2 Timothy.

First, Paul says in 2 Timothy 1:8-10: ". . . God, who hath saved us, and called us with an holy calling, not according to our works, but according to his own purpose and grace, which was given us in Christ Jesus before the world began, but is now made manifest by the appearing of our Saviour Jesus Christ, who hath abolished death, and hath brought life and immortality to light through the gospel."

In that passage we have the record of His first appearing, the shining forth when He came into the world to abolish death by His death and resurrection.

Then, the apostle in one of those moving and wonderful doxologies, said in 1 Timothy 6:13-16: "I give thee charge in the sight of God, who quickeneth all things, and before Christ Jesus, who before Pontius Pilate witnessed a good confession; that thou keep this commandment without spot, unrebukeable, until the appearing of our Lord Jesus Christ."

Paul speaks of the second appearing, when Christ "shall shew, who is the blessed and only Potentate, the King of kings, and Lord of lords; Who only hath immortality, dwelling in the light which no man can approach unto; whom no man hath seen, nor can see: to whom be honour and power everlasting. Amen."

When I read something like this given us by the apostle Paul, it makes me think of a skylark or a meadowlark mounting a branch and bursting into an unexpected but brilliantly melodious song. Paul often breaks forth with one of his wonderful and uplifting ascriptions of praise to Jesus Christ in the midst of his epistles, and this is one of those!

Paul reminds Christian believers here that when Jesus Christ appears again, He will show forth, and leave no doubts at all as to the Person of the King of kings and Lord of lords.

Paul was also careful to comfort those in the early church who feared that they might die before this second appearing of Jesus Christ. Actually, there were believers in the Thessalonian church who were worried on two counts, the first of which was their thought that the Lord had already come and they had been passed by. The second was their thought that they would die before He came and that through death, they would miss out on the joys of His appearing.

So, Paul wrote the two epistles to the Thessalonian church to straighten them out on the truth concerning Christ's second appearing.

"If we believe that Jesus died and rose again, even so them also which sleep in Jesus will God bring with him"—that is, if you die and go to be with the Lord, God will bring you along with Jesus at His appearing—"for this we say unto you by the word of the Lord, that we which are alive and remain unto the coming of the Lord shall not (run ahead of those) which are asleep. For the Lord himself shall descend from heaven with a shout, with the voice of the archangel, and with the trump of God: and the dead in Christ shall rise first: Then we which are alive and remain shall be caught up together with them in the clouds, to meet the Lord in the air: and so shall we ever be with the Lord. Wherefore comfort one another with these words."

You see, Paul's inspired explanation instructs us that those who died before the coming of Jesus will not be at a disadvantage. If anything, they will be in a position of advantage, because before the Lord glorifies the waiting saints throughout the earth, He will raise in glorified bodies the great company of believers who have been parted from us by death throughout the centuries.

Brethren, that is very plainly what the apostle Paul tells

us in the instructions originally given to the Thessalonian Christians.

Don't we have the right to think that it is very strange that the majority of the Christian pulpits are completely silent concerning this glorious truth of the imminent return of Jesus Christ? It is paradoxical that there should be this great silence in Christian churches at the very time when the danger of suddenly being swept off the face of the earth is greater than it has ever been.

Russia and the United States, the two great nuclear powers, continue to measure their ability to destroy in terms of *over-kill*. This is a terrible compound word never before used in the history of the English language. The scientists had to express the almost incredible destructive power of the nuclear bombs in our stockpiles—so the word *over-kill* is a new invention of our times.

Both the United States and Russia have made statements about the over-kill power of nuclear stockpiles suffcient to kill every man, woman and child in the world—not once, but 20 times over. That is over-kill!

Isn't it just like that old enemy, Satan, to persuade the saints in the Body of Christ to engage in bitter arguments about post-tribulation rapture and pre-tribulation rapture; post-millennialism, a-millennialism and pre-millennialism—right at the very hour when over-kill hangs over us like a black, threatening cloud.

Brethren, this is the kind of age and hour when the Lord's people should be so alert to the hope and promise of His coming that they should get up every morning just like a child on Christmas morning—eager and believing that it should be today!

Instead of that kind of expectancy, what do we find throughout His church today? Arguments pro and con about His coming, about the details of the rapture—and some of this to the point of bitterness. Otherwise, we find great segments of Christians who seem to be able to blithely ignore the whole matter of the return of Jesus Christ.

Very few ministers bother to preach from the Book of Revelation any more—and that is true of large areas of evangelicalism and fundamentalism, too! We have been intimidated by the cynicism and sophistication of our day.

There are so many apparent anomalies and contradictions in society and in the ranks of professing Christians that someone will certainly write a book about it.

There is the anomaly of the necessity of getting to know one another better in order to love and understand one another better. Millions are traveling and meeting other millions and getting acquainted, so if the premise is true, we ought all to love each other like one big blessed family.

Instead, we hate each other like the devil. It is true that all over the world the nations are hating each other in startling, record-breaking measure.

I will mention another contradiction that is all too apparent. Our educators and sociologists told us that all we had to do was allow the teaching of sexual education in the schools and all of our vexing sexual problems in society would disappear.

Is it not a strange anomaly that the generation that has been teaching and outlining more about sexual practices than any twenty-five generations combined did in the past is the generation that is the most rotten and perverted in sexual conduct?

And is it not strange, too, that the very generation that might expect to be atomized suddenly by over-kill is the generation that is afraid to talk about the coming of the Lord and unwilling to discuss His gracious promises of deliverance and glorification?

You may not expect me to say it, but I will: what a bunch of weirdies we are! What a strange generation we are!

God has said that He would place a great premium on the holy, spiritual consistency of the Christian saints, but how inconsistent we are when we allow the devil and our own carnality to confuse and mix us up so that we will be diverted from patient waiting for His appearing!

So, we live between two mighty events—that of His incarnation, death and resurrection, and that of His ultimate appearing and the glorification of those He died to save. This is the interim time for the saints—but it is not a vacuum. He has given us much to do and He asks for our faithfulness.

In the meantime, we are zealous of good works, living soberly, righteously, godly in this present world, looking unto Him and His promise. In the midst of our lives, and between the two great mountain peaks of God's acts in the world, we look back and remember, and we look forward and hope! As members of His own loving fellowship, we break the bread and drink the wine. We sing His praise and we pray in His Name, remembering and expecting!

Brethren, that moves me more than anything else in this world. It is such a blessed privilege that it is more beautiful and satisfying than friendships or paintings or sunsets or any other beauties of nature. Looking back to His grace and love; looking forward to His coming and glory; meanwhile actively working and joyously hoping—until He comes!

Excerpt from
Paths to Power

Miracles Follow the Plow

51

Miracles Follow the Plow

*Break up your fallow ground: for it is time to seek the
Lord, till he come and rain righteousness upon you.*
—Hos. 10:12

Here are two kinds of ground: fallow ground, and ground
that has been broken up by the plow.

The fallow field is smug, contented, protected from the
shock of the plow and the agitation of the harrow. Such a
field, as it lies year after year, becomes a familiar landmark to the crow and the blue jay. Had it intelligence, it
might take a lot of satisfaction in its reputation; it has sta-
bility; nature has adopted it; it can be counted upon to
remain always the same while the fields around it change
from brown to green and back to brown again. Safe and
undisturbed, it sprawls lazily in the sunshine, the picture
of sleepy contentment. But it is paying a terrible price for
its tranquility: Never does it see the miracle of growth;
never does it feel the motions of mounting life nor see the
wonders of bursting seed nor the beauty of ripening grain.
Fruit it can never know because it is afraid of the plow
and the harrow.

In direct opposite to this, the cultivated field has yielded
itself to the adventure of living. The protecting fence has
opened to admit the plow, and the plow has come as
plows always come, practical, cruel, business-like and in a
hurry. Peace has been shattered by the shouting farmer
and the rattle of machinery. The field has felt the travail

of change; it has been upset, turned over, bruised and broken, but its rewards come hard upon its labors. The seed shoots up into the daylight its miracle of life, curious, exploring the new world above it. All over the field the hand of God is at work in the age-old and ever renewed service of creation. New things are born, to grow, mature, and consummate the grand prophecy latent in the seed when it entered the ground. Nature's wonders follow the plow.

There are two kinds of lives also: the fallow and the plowed. For examples of the fallow life we need not go far. They are all too plentiful among us.

The man of fallow life is contented with himself and the fruit he once bore. He does not want to be disturbed. He smiles in tolerant superiority at revivals, fastings, self-searchings, and all the travail of fruit-bearing and the anguish of advance. The spirit of adventure is dead within him. He is steady, "faithful," always in his accustomed place (like the old field), conservative, and something of a landmark in the little church. But he is fruitless. The curse of such a life is that it is fixed, both in size and in content. *To be* has taken the place of *to become*. The worst that can be said of such a man is that he *is* what he *will be*. He has fenced himself in, and by the same act, he has fenced out God and the miracle.

The plowed life is the life that has, in the act of repentance, thrown down the protecting fences and sent the plow of confession into the soul. The urge of the Spirit, the pressure of circumstances and the distress of fruitless living have combined thoroughly to humble the heart. Such a life has put away defense, and has forsaken the safety of death for the peril of life. Discontent, yearning, contrition, courageous obedience to the will of God: these have bruised and broken the soil till it is ready again for the seed. And as always fruit follows the plow. Life and growth begin as God "rains down righteousness." Such a one can testify, "And the hand of the Lord was upon me there."

Corresponding to these two kinds of life, religious history shows two phases, the dynamic and the static.

The dynamic periods were those heroic times when God's people stirred themselves to do the Lord's bidding and went out fearlessly to carry His witness to the world. They exchanged the safety of inaction for the hazards of God-inspired progress. Invariably the power of God followed such action. The miracle of God went when and where His people went; it stayed when His people stopped.

The static periods were those times when the people of God tired of the struggle and sought a life of peace and security. Then they busied themselves trying to conserve the gains made in those more daring times when the power of God moved among them.

Bible history is replete with examples. Abraham "went out" on his great adventure of faith, and God went with him. Revelations, theophanies, the gift of Palestine, covenants and promises of rich blessings to come were the result. Then Israel went down into Egypt, and the wonders ceased for four hundred years. At the end of that time Moses heard the call of God and stepped forth to challenge the oppressor. A whirlwind of power accompanied that challenge, and Israel soon began to march. As long as she dared to march, God sent out His miracles to clear the way for her. Whenever she lay down like a fallow field, He turned off His blessing and waited for her to rise again and command His power.

This is a brief but fair outline of the history of Israel and of the Church as well. As long as they "went forth and preached everywhere," the Lord worked "with them. . . . confirming the word with signs following." But when they retreated to monasteries or played at building pretty cathedrals, the help of God was withdrawn till a Luther or a Wesley arose to challenge hell again. Then invariably God poured out His power as before.

In every denomination, missionary society, local church

or individual Christian this law operates. God works as long as His people *live daringly:* He ceases when they no longer need His aid. As soon as we seek protection outside of God, we find it to our own undoing. Let us build a safety-wall of endowments, by-laws, prestige, multiplied agencies for the delegation of our duties, and creeping paralysis sets in at once, a paralysis which can only end in death.

The power of God comes only where it is called out by the plow. It is released into the Church only when she is doing something that demands it. By the word "doing" I do not mean mere activity. The Church has plenty of "hustle" as it is, but in all her activities she is very careful to leave her fallow ground mostly untouched. She is careful to confine her hustling within the fear-marked boundaries of complete safety. That is why she is fruitless; she is safe, but fallow.

Look around today and see where the miracles of power are taking place. Never in the seminary where each thought is prepared for the student, to be received painlessly and at second hand; never in the religious institution where tradition and habit have long ago made faith unnecessary; never in the old church where memorial tablets plastered over the furniture bear silent testimony to a glory that once was. Invariably where daring faith is struggling to advance against hopeless odds, there is God sending "help from the sanctuary."

In the missionary society with which I have for many years been associated, I have noticed that the power of God has always hovered over our frontiers. Miracles have accompanied our advances and have ceased when and where we allowed ourselves to become satisfied and ceased to advance. The creed of power cannot save a movement from barrenness. There must be also the work of power.

But I am more concerned with the effect of this truth upon the local church and the individual. Look at that church where plentiful fruit was once the regular and expected thing, but now there is little or no fruit, and the power of God seems to be in abeyance. What is the trouble? God has not changed, nor has His purpose for that church changed in the slightest measure. No, the church itself has changed.

A little self-examination will reveal that it and its members have become fallow. It has lived through its early travails and has now come to accept an easier way of life. It is content to carry on its painless program with enough money to pay its bills and a membership large enough to assure its future. Its members now look to it for security rather than for guidance in the battle between good and evil. It has become a school instead of a barracks. Its members are students, not soldiers. They study the experiences of others instead of seeking new experiences of their own.

The only way to power for such a church is to come out of hiding and once more take the danger-encircled path of obedience. Its security is its deadliest foe. The church that fears the plow writes its own epitaph: the church that uses the plow walks in the way of revival.

Excerpt from
Let My People Go

The Jaffray Pattern

52

The Jaffray Pattern

Right here seems as good a place as any to look at the Jaffray philosophy of Christian missions. It was a simple philosophy based on New Testament principles and shot through with salty common sense. From it he evolved a pattern for his work, a pattern whose lines show through everything he did from his earliest South China days to the end of his life.

Whether Robert Jaffray ever sat down and reasoned out a policy is very doubtful. His mind did not work that way. He scooped his ideas on the move as a swallow at evening takes its supper on the wing. The Bible and a sound instinct guided him, and hard experience soon corrected any flaws in his theories. His views were never complex nor difficult to comprehend. The work of missions was fairly simple after all. It consisted chiefly of four things to do: contact, evangelize, organize and instruct. That was all. But in the doing of these essentials a man might toil a lifetime, and his toil would be fruitful, for these were the things Christ had sent His servants to do.

Contact was first. Nothing could be done until communication had been established. The missionary must go to the lost tribes. This was the basal tenet in his missionary creed, and to him it was the voice of command. It created within his mind an eager restlessness that never left him for one day nor one hour while life remained in him. The sight of a map or the sound of a strange heathen name

stirred him as the sound of an alarm bell stirred the old
fire horse of other days. So Jaffray was a pioneer, an ex-
plorer, an adventurer obsessed with the urge to discover
new peoples and hidden tribes.

It is this aspect of missionary work that captures the
imagination of the public. We are all children enough to
love the thrill of missionary adventure enjoyed by proxy,
and Jaffray knew this. As a good showman he was willing
to give the people at home what they wanted. His news-
letters and magazine articles often read like real tales of
the wild, but they were never told for their own sake
nor for mere amusement. Jaffray was altogether too serious for any such child's play. If he could win attention
with honest reports of exotic customs and curious ways of
strange peoples, he was not adverse to doing it, but always
his motives were in full view. He wanted help. He wanted
money, lots of it, but more than all, he wanted young men
to hurry over and help him with the job. And they came,
these young men, and they came winged with prayer and
backed with the consecrated wealth of the people at home.

After contact came evangelization. Christ had told His
disciples to go into all the world and make disciples. To
Jaffray that could mean only one thing: win lost men to
Christ now, bring them to trust Him as their personal Saviour at once, without waiting for civilizing influences or
long courses of instruction to condition them. They had
but to hear the Gospel and they could be saved, as certainly
as any white man could.

That was Jaffray's theory, and its soundness was confirmed in man-to-man practice. It worked, that was the
glory of it. Lives were actually changed overnight, transformed by this simple technique. Men could and did jump
from raw savagery into the kingdom of God at one bound,
and for the most part, those who made the great transition
lived to prove that the change was real and permanent.

The next step was to organize these new Christians into
a church. It would need to be a simple thing at first, little

more than a loose, common-consent kind of organization with certain men among them picked to act as leaders and give some direction to the group. Later it could go on to a more perfect form of organization with a pastor, deacons and elders; but that could wait, for the missionary would act as the real leader until the new converts had been better instructed. Ecclesiastical-minded persons may smile at this, but it worked, and it still works, and that fact cannot be smiled away.

Then, this new church must be taught the great truths of the Christian faith, must be instructed, indoctrinated, and to accomplish this two means were required: the school and the printing press. These came after organization, and where Jaffray could have his way, not long after.

The printing press was to Jaffray what hand-written epistles were to Paul, a means of keeping in touch with his converts as they increased in number, and distances made personal contact impossible. Then too, the press made available to these new Christians the best in spiritual literature. Usually Jaffray's presses turned out matter written by himself and addressed to particular needs, but they produced also books, tracts, magazines, Bible courses, and expositions of one after another of the books of the Bible as he could prepare them and as he felt the people were ready to receive them.

Along with the printing press stood the Bible School as an effective instrument for the dissemination of the truth. Jaffray believed in the Bible School with a positiveness amounting to sheer dogmatism. He knew its power and promoted it with unremitting zeal. Foreign missionaries would never be the last word in the evangelization of any country. The best and swiftest work would always be done by Christian nationals operating among their own people. But these must first be taught the truth and trained for the most effective service. The Bible School could do this; there was no other agent that could. So every field must have a school; at least one, and more if the need demanded. That was Jaffray's view, and again its soundness was confirmed in practical outwork.

The speed with which the Christian faith spread among the hitherto unreached peoples testifies to the fact that Jaffray's vision was divinely given. He would never allow his workers to huddle together; they were expected to spread out, always spread out and stay on the move. He was so insistent upon this that some of his workers were at times led to question his wisdom, and a few dared to oppose him outright. Usually subsequent developments justified him, however, and the doubters were forced to acknowledge that he had been right.

"Of course," said one official before whom he appeared to request permission to preach the Gospel within his territory, "of course you will concentrate your forces?"

"Certainly," agreed Jaffray quickly. Then stepping to the wall where hung a huge map of the country, he touched with his finger one after another spot on the map.

"We'll concentrate here, and here, and here, and here."

"Why, how many missionaries have you?" asked the astonished official.

"Six," replied Jaffray, unsmiling.

It was this strategy of "concentrating" all over the map that gave such thrust to his missionary drives.

In spite, however, of this blitz-like speed of advance he never fell into the error current today in some quarters— he never believed he had done the Lord's work merely by announcing the Gospel and moving on. He would not leave the new Christians to fall back into heathenism. Wherever a few converts were made, there a church must be formed; gains must be consolidated. Then the messenger could go on, but not till then. This was wisdom and it was New Testament procedure. It might well serve as a pattern for all missionary societies everywhere.

The notion that we have only to announce the Gospel once to each tribe and then pass on to the next without regard to results is as old as it is false. Though it is the philosophy back of much present-day missionary enterprise, it is nevertheless a plain heresy of method based upon a misreading of orders. It is interesting to know that Wesley and his Methodists had this to face in their early missionary activities, and it is instructive to learn how they handled it.

In one section of the old Methodist Discipline published in 1848 and bearing (I would guess) from an earlier day the marks of Wesley's own mind, under the head, "Rules by which we should Continue, or Desist from, Preaching at any Place," the question is asked, "Is it advisable for us to preach in as many places as we can without forming any societies?" The answer is emphatic. "By no means. We have made the trail in various places; and that for considerable time. But all the seed has fallen by the wayside. There is scarcely any fruit remaining."

Jaffray was of Presbyterian stock, and it is doubtful whether he ever gave much attention to the ways of the early Methodists, but in the hot fires of experience he learned the same lessons they had learned before him and he arrived at the same conclusions. This may not be the last word that can be spoken on the subject, but the wise missionary will listen respectfully to these masters. They bring to the support of their philosophy the unanswerable argument of overwhelming success.